Personal Takeover

Personal Takeover

Create a Professional Life Full of Optimism, Energy, and Impact

by

Gary Gabel

CAREER PRESS

Franklin Lakes, NJ

Personal Takeover
EDITED BY CLAYTON W. LEADBETTER
TYPESET BY JOHN J. O'SULLIVAN
Cover design by Design Concept
Printed in the U.S.A. by Book-mart Press

To order this title, please call toll-free 1-800-CAREER-1 (NJ and Canada: 201-848-0310) to order using VISA or MasterCard, or for further information on books from Career Press.

The Career Press, Inc., 3 Tice Road, PO Box 687,
Franklin Lakes, NJ 07417

www.careerpress.com

Library of Congress Cataloging-in-Publication Data

Gabel, Gary.
    Personal takeover : create a professional life full of optimisn, energy, and impact / by Gary Gabel.
       p. cm.
    Includes bibliographical references (p.) and index.
    ISBN 1-56414-646-4 (paper)
       1. Success—Psychological aspects. 2. Success in business. I. Title.
    BF637.S8 .G29 2003
    158—dc21   2002031567

Acknowledgments

A lot of people have helped in the creation of *Personal Takeover*. Many have volunteered to read the various drafts and have given excellent critique. Among them, special thanks go to Tom Buck and Lisa Martin. Others have provided their personal stories to help illustrate the points I've made throughout.

In particular, I wish to thank my wife, Lisa, for her support during this process and Bruce Wexler for his editorial help. I'd like to thank my editors at Career Press, Mike Lewis, for seeing the power of the personal takeover concept, along with Stacey Farkas and Clayton Leadbetter, for helping me bring the concept to life in book form.

One of the individuals referred to in the text of *Personal Takeover* is Leonard E. Read, former President and founder of the Foundation for Economic Education. The Foundation has done much to foster a better understanding of the ideas of free markets and limited government, an important cornerstone of takeover thinking. The Foundation is located in Irvington-on-Hudson, New York.

Contents

Introduction

STANLEY WAS SITTING IN HIS OFFICE, PAYING ABSOLUTELY NO attention to the fact that it was 11 a.m. and he hadn't done a lick of work. Out of the corner of his eye, he noticed a recent customer survey he'd just received. He picked it up, looked at it, rolled his eyes, crumpled it up, and took a shot at the wastebasket in the corner. He was a young executive with Cardy Restaurant Supply. Frank Cardy had built the company from nothing, and today his warehouse supplied a quarter of the restaurants and hotels within a 50-mile radius. Stanley had joined the company a few years ago after receiving his M.B.A. It wasn't his first choice; he'd applied to just about every Fortune 500 company in the area and settled for working for Cardy because it was the only offer he received. Stanley was the first M.B.A. ever hired by Cardy because someone had told them, "You need M.B.A.s. These people are really smart." Bob Bujarski, one of the warehouse workers, had summed up his assessment of Stanley's contribution to the company when he quipped, "I think Personnel used the ashtray test when they hired this guy. They put an ashtray under Stanley's nose, and when it fogged up, they said, 'You're hired.'" Stanley figured he'd only stay for one year or two at the most, but now he was in his fourth year with the company, and bigger corporations weren't beating down the door to hire him.

It was Monday, the weekend was over, but Stanley was not yet prepared to face the fact that the work-week had begun. Therefore, he was happy when Bruno, a member of his work team, entered his office and sat down on the other side of the desk. They were supposed to be working with other team members to develop an improved customer delivery process based on the recent survey, but Stanley was talking about everything except work.

"I was playing football over the weekend, and man, I was in the zone," said Stanley. "You know what I mean, Bruno? The zone?"

Bruno looked at him. "Yeah, sure. You were playing well."

"More than well. I was the quarterback, and I felt like I was in a trance. Every pass I threw, *wham*, right in the hands of my receivers. I even scrambled and ran for two touchdowns myself. What a feeling! That's what I meant when I said I was in the zone, Bruno. Like Joe Montana, when he was at his best. I was completely in control."

Bruno nodded but didn't say anything. He had at first been a little intimidated by Stanley, because he had received his M.B.A. at a prestigious university, while Bruno had worked his way up and was taking classes at the local community college. In recent months, the feeling of intimidation was being replaced by disgust, as Bruno saw how little Stanley accomplished.

"Imagine the possibilities," Stanley said. "Think about what it would be like to always feel like that, like you were able to control your fate and weren't always at everyone else's beck and call."

"You mean like having John giving us our assignments," Bruno said. John was the head of their team.

"Not only John, but all the bosses who decide when we get a raise, how much of a bonus we receive, when we can take vacations, how long we have for lunch."

Just then, Sally from Logistics, who had been assigned to their team, stuck her head in the door. She was two years younger than both of them, but it was clear to everyone that she was a rising star. As usual, she didn't have time to sit down and shoot the breeze. "Hi guys. Just thought I'd give you a heads up that John wants to meet this afternoon; you'll get an e-mail about it pretty soon. Which is why I hope you'll take a few minutes to look at this." Sally handed them each a piece of paper that outlined a strategy for increasing customer delivery speed. "I came up with this last night, and if you guys agree with it, maybe you can add some of your ideas and we can present it together. I'll check in with you before the meeting."

Seconds after she left, Stanley dropped her paper on his desk as if it were tainted. "What's wrong with her? She's always coming through like that, always trying some new idea, always acting so gung ho."

"I don't know. Maybe *she's* in the zone," said Bruno, mocking Stanley's earlier statement.

Stanley looked at him with surprise and considered his observation, then shook his head. "She's not in any zone. She's just a suck-up. That's why the bosses like her."

"She always seems to be here working before you get in and after you leave."

Stanley thought a moment. "That just makes my point, Bruno."

"She's a suck-up because she works hard?"

"Well, yeah. They just want us to work harder around here so management can get rich."

"Well, we got pretty nice bonuses last year."

"Nice is a relative term. We get pennies, they get millions. Look Bruno, they're just trying to brainwash you with all that talk of how everyone benefits from great new ideas. You and I are never going to make as much as John and all the other higher-ups."

"Sally might."

"Sure, but that's because she's a woman and they need more women in management for political correctness. Face it, Bruno, we're being taken advantage of and there's not a thing we can do about it."

Later, Sally returned to Stanley's office with Bruno in tow. Sally asked them if they had given any thought to the ideas she'd outlined, and to Stanley's surprise, Bruno suddenly began drawing a diagram on the whiteboard and sharing some intriguing thoughts about how they could employ a new information-sharing system devised by one of their vendors to accelerate delivery times. Sally seemed impressed by his idea, but she was upset that Stanley hadn't even bothered to come up with a single new thought.

"Stanley," she said, "you're probably one of the brighter people I've met, but you're also one of the laziest."

"I'm not lazy. I'm just not a suck-up like you two."

She looked at Stanley and shook her head. "Stanley, Bruno's not a suck up and neither am I. When are you going to stop acting like the world's against you? You act like you're a victim."

"We're all victims."

"Well, I don't feel like a victim. I like my life, and I like what I do."

Stanley hesitated a moment and then replied, "You really are a victim, but you've put a face on top of it, so you don't quite think you are. It's just like putting on makeup. You've covered up your true thoughts about what's going on."

Sally was dumbfounded. "How can your view be so warped that you can't even give me the benefit of knowing what I truly believe?"

Before Stanley could reply, Bruno looked at him and said, "You know, in the three years that you've worked here, the only time I've ever seen you positive and excited about anything was earlier today when you talked about how you were in the zone when you were playing football."

"So? What's that got to do with anything?"

"I guess what it has to do with is that you think it's only possible to be in control and have an impact once in a blue moon when you're playing football. If that were true, it makes sense that you would always be cynical and pessimistic. But what if you're wrong? What if it were possible to be in charge of your life all the time, and you just didn't know it? And imagine if you'd spent 10 years like this instead of four. Or 20 years or your whole career. If you'd been sure you were helpless and powerless, but in reality you could have been in complete control, what a waste your life would have been."

Bruno just figured out what it takes some people a lifetime to learn: *We all possess the power to take control over our own lives*. Many of us, like Stanley, don't see it, but we all possess the power. Call it being in the zone, self-empowerment, or positive thinking. Those terms, however, don't quite get at the depth of the opportunity open to everyone. A more apt term is **Personal Takeover**. Just as people can take over organizations and assume the power and control over those organizations, we can launch personal takeovers that provide us with the same power and control over our own lives.

People like Stanley never attempt personal takeovers. For them, the week is tedium and the weekend is the only time they really enjoy their lives. They're victims, and it is easy to feel victimized in today's world. There are so many things out of our control, we feel like we're helpless and our view of the future is overshadowed with pessimism.

Just look at the rate of change. Every decade provides more changes in the world than the previous one. With the proliferation of the Internet, along with the plummeting price of computers, we have become privy to more information at a faster pace. This information allows markets to be served more rapidly and allows competition to appear anywhere in the world. We have gone to a world economy where tennis shoes are made in China and cars are made in Korea. A decision can be made in Germany today that directly affects you tomorrow.

With all of this rapid change and intense competition comes the inevitable fact that organizations will grow and decline more rapidly than ever before. Since the early 1980s, over 20 million people have lost their jobs due to structural changes in our economy. Downsizing increased in the early 90s, only to be replaced by aggressive recruitment as the U.S. experienced unprecedented growth at the end of the decade, followed by aggressive layoffs with the dot-com bust and general market softening. As of this writing, the economy seems to be floundering, and many people have seen their wealth cut in half in the stock market. It's likely that we're going to experience continued volatility, and this volatility will foster the illusion that we have no control.

Decisions are made that affect us but seem out of our control. It is easy to feel quite helpless in such a transient world—one where suddenly the World Trade Center collapses. When faced with a tumultuous environment, we naturally feel like victims. Yet, there are some people like Sally, who seem to thrive in all of this turmoil.

In the following pages, you'll find stories of other individuals who were able to take over their lives despite the change and even chaos that surrounded them. You'll also find plenty of examples of others whose views of the world around them have actually kept them from succeeding. The process and accompanying tools presented here will help you develop a takeover mindset and join the ranks of those like Sally, who have chosen a path of personal takeover. This takeover mindset is the direct opposite of what I call the victim mindset, where people feel as if their ability to choose and direct their life has been taken away from them. People like Stanley are perfectly capable of taking back control of their jobs and careers but refuse to believe that it's possible to do so. Pessimism, cynicism, and fatalism are typical reactions to the rapid change we are all experiencing as we enter the 21st century, and they distort our perspective of our environments.

Over the years, I've observed a wide variety of people make the transition from a victim to a takeover mindset. From young corporate executives to older entrepreneurs, these individuals have discovered that they can take charge of their jobs and careers no matter what their circumstances. It doesn't matter if they have a tyrant of a boss or if they don't have the most marketable job skills or if they have struggled in their own businesses. It doesn't make a difference if they're clinging to their jobs by a thread, if the economy is bad, or if their company is on shaky ground. The whole point of a takeover mindset is that you're in control; that you have a choice in the direction of your life. What is going on inside your mind will have a greater impact on your future than all the external events going on in your life.

I should caution you that this isn't simply a matter of adopting a positive mental attitude or saying to yourself, "I'm in control!" You can't launch a personal takeover overnight. It's a process, and the techniques that are part of it require practice. You need to learn new ways of looking at things as well as new ways of doing things; you also have to unlearn a lot of the ideas that come with victim thinking.

So expect to do some work, but also expect to find fun and challenge in the process. Above all else, recognize that a personal takeover can help you achieve ambitious goals that you might have previously been afraid to even think about because they seemed so out of reach. Goals such as achieving capstone positions, starting your own company, or switching careers are all attainable once you oust your de facto board of directors and assume the top spot. Just as significantly, when you're in charge, your entire quality of work life will improve. No more dreading waking up and going to the office on Monday morning. No more clock-watching during the day. When you take back control of your life, you can begin feeling infinitely better about what you're doing because you recognize the things you're doing for yourself. The boredom and fear that are too often part of the work day are greatly diminished when you're not at the mercy of forces beyond your control.

So get ready to start the takeover, beginning with a shift in how you view reality.

Chapter 1

You Create Your Own Reality

" " *I thought you were my heaven;*
but it's pretty hot all of a sudden."

Y OU ARE WHERE YOU ARE TODAY BECAUSE OF THE CHOICES YOU have made. No matter how much it may appear that things just sort of happened to you, the fact is that you made a choice each time something happened, and that choice led you in a specific direction. These choices have been made because of the way you perceive the world around you. The world you perceive could be one filled with hope and opportunity, or it could be a dead end, where people are lurking around every corner, just waiting to take advantage of you.

You create your own reality. That reality could be positive or negative, but it's yours. The person who lives next door has a different reality than you. Your fellow worker in the next workstation also has a different reality than you. Your perceived reality can be a prison; it can limit your thoughts and behaviors in ways that keep you stuck; or your reality can be filled with opportunity and abundance.

You are governed by your perceptions in numerous ways. Consider whether you've ever placed limits on what you can do based on how you viewed reality. Have you ever made any of the following statements (or ones similar to them):

- I can't leave this job because I'll never find another one that pays the same.
- I'm not smart enough to get a job in management.
- It's impossible for me to switch fields at my age.
- Only brown-nosers get ahead at this company.
- My boss never takes my ideas seriously, so I'm not going to bother coming up with anything.
- I can't sell.
- I know what I'd love to do, but no one would ever give me the opportunity to do that type of work.

None of these things may be true, but they *seem* true, and as a result, they might as well be reality. Put another way, reality is objective, but our interpretation of that reality is subjective. This can be difficult to accept because many of us believe that our interpretation of reality is the correct one. In an objective reality, a chair is a chair. "A" is "A." There are certain absolute truths, and these truths are not altered by our desires for them not to be true. Assume your friend, Lisa, has just purchased a black leather chair and invites you over to see it. You are likely going to see the same thing that she sees. If Lisa were to ask you what you see, you'd probably respond, "a black leather chair," and if she were to ask you to estimate the size, your estimate would probably not be far from hers. If you were to both measure the chair, your measurements would likely be equal. In essence, not only is a chair a chair, but most of us see this physical object in a similar light. One person's experience is very similar to another's.

Objective reality doesn't apply to intangibles

We mistakenly translate that same objective reality from the physical world into the world of esthetics, action, intention, emotion, and communication. For instance, the objective reality that a chair is a chair gives us a feeling of being stable and grounded. It is important for us to believe that the chair we see today is going to be the same tomorrow—that it's not going to suddenly dissolve or transform itself into a double-dutch apple pie. It allows us to feel that we can depend on something. We can rely on ourselves and our own understanding of reality.

Scenario

When we turn our focus toward esthetic appreciation of the chair, our realities might be quite different. Tracy walks into Lisa's house and spies the new black leather chair.

"Got a new chair, huh?"

"Yeah, isn't it great? I love leather."

"It's a bit too cold for me—and I find the black color so masculine."

"Really?"

"Yeah, I like flowery print things."

Lisa is puzzled. "Then why did you wallpaper your front room in leopard skin?"

"I want to go to Africa, and it reminds me of my plans."

"So, you don't like my chair."

"It's actually pretty gross."

"Pretty gross?"

"It's just so big and leathery!"

Lisa is now becoming exasperated with Tracy's interpretation of her chair.

"Okay, let's change the subject."

"You know, it might not even be a chair," continues Tracy. "It might be a loveseat. Yeah, that's what I think it is—a loveseat! You'd never buy a chair that big. And all that leather."

"Tracy, shut up."

The fact is, when it comes to the world of esthetics, emotions, communications, and personal relations, reality is made up of interpretations. Tracy and Lisa both see the same chair, but their interpretations of the chair, or how they see it, are quite different. We are continually surprised by other people's actions. Over the course of years, each of us develops our own view of reality, and we are absolutely sure that our view of reality is correct. Unless, of course, somebody comes along to challenge that view. Then we are surprised.

Thinking outside the circle

Leonard E. Read, philosopher and economist, once said that when he was a teenage boy, the knowledge he possessed could be represented by a small circle, as shown below. Everything he knew could be held within that circle. Therefore, he believed he knew a lot, because if one were to measure the circumference of the circle, all of the space outside of the circle was relatively minor. He concluded, logically, that there was relatively little he didn't know.

As he grew older, Read's circle of knowledge expanded, so that by the time he reached his 60s his circle was five times as large, as shown in the following figure. Now he possessed five times the amount of knowledge he had as a young man.

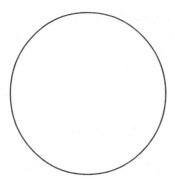

The space outside his new circle, however, was significantly larger, representing the huge amount of knowledge outside Read's world. Leonard Read realized in his later years that he had made many false assumptions on the nature of reality. This recognition is wisdom. Wisdom comes from understanding what we don't know and realizing that everything is not black and white.

The problem, of course, is that this wisdom often comes only with age and experience. Think about all the certainties you had when you were younger. In high school you might have been convinced that people who were handsome or pretty had it made and never had any problems. In college, you may have been absolutely sure that capitalism was a fatally flawed system and socialism was the only viable means of governing people. As a young business person, you may have been absolutely sure that the key to success was adopting the right style—the right clothes or the right club memberships. If someone challenged your view of reality, you would have argued strenuously that your perception was correct.

My daughter, Christina, is a good example. When she became a teenager, we found that we disagreed on even the most minor points. I think it began at age 13. Well, the more I think about it, it might have begun at age three. One day, when she was 18 years old, I had a discussion with her and said, "You know, Christina, I'll bet that when you are 30 years old you'll probably say to me, 'Dad, some of the time you actually were right.'" Christina looked aghast and said, "Dad, that's never going to happen!"

Over time, we each come to certain conclusions about reality, and these conclusions tend to stay fixed until such time as those views are challenged. Take a look at the picture in the figure that follows. Assume that this symbolically represents your view of reality. In the center, you have a core. A series of lines come out from the core. Two elliptical lines appear to surround the center. At least they look like two elliptical lines, but if you were to take a straight edge and lay it along those elliptical lines, you would find that the lines actually are straight. Your picture of reality was incorrect. Further evidence has shown that those lines aren't as you originally perceived them.

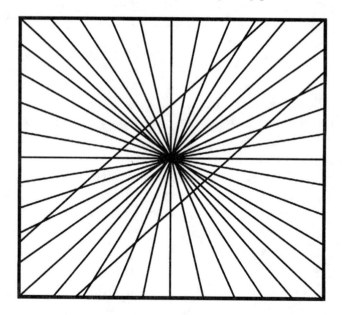

The picture of reality we hold is often the same as in this image. We believe that our views about ourselves, others, work, and success, in general, sit on a solid foundation. Upon further inspection, though, many of us will find that a number of our beliefs may actually hinder our ability to achieve success, instead of promoting it. We believe that our individual picture of reality is going to lead to success, yet we may actually be working against our own purposes.

Here is another example. Look at the following figure and think about what you see.

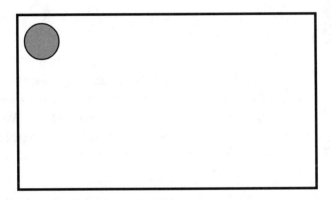

Did you see a dot in the upper left-hand corner? If so, you have seen what most people see when I conduct this experiment in seminars. Your focus is on the dot when, in fact, what also exists is a huge white rectangle. We often focus on one small piece, and in many instances when it comes to organizational life, that one piece is a negative one.

Scenario

Kim, the Human Resources Director for a service company, is conducting an exit interview with Karen, an employee who has turned in her resignation.

"I can't take this place anymore," says Karen. "I've got to get out."

"Why, what happened?"

"People are abusive around here. The way they talk to you is ridiculous."

"Are the other employees in your call center treating you poorly?"

"No, no, no. They're a great group."

"Well, is it your boss, Caroline, who's treating you poorly?"

"No, she's a great boss. We get along really well."

"Is the problem with our management team or our President?"

"No, I think they're doing a great job. And the President is quite personable."

"Well, then I'm confused. Where's the problem?"

"I have to work with this account manager, Elaine, and I really don't like the way she talks down to me. She'll come up to me at 4:45 on a Friday and say, 'We'll have to work this weekend to get this job out.' No planning, and then we have to cover for her. And she isn't even polite about it!"

Karen has allowed the behavior of one person to overshadow what might otherwise be a very positive work experience. She has created her own negative reality. She is convinced that the organization is abusive based on generalizing her experience with Elaine instead of considering the many others who are not abusive at all. In other words, she is focusing on the dot.

Three basic takeover rules

In this chapter, I'll introduce three basic takeover rules. By accepting these rules, or basic premises, you provide a foundation for your own personal takeover. Throughout the book, I'll expand upon this initial list of three, so that by the end you'll have a number of rules to help you as you embark upon your own personal takeover or help someone else achieve theirs.

A personal takeover isn't possible if you're convinced that your interpretation of reality is fixed and absolute. If, on the other hand, you're willing to accept that your interpretation of reality is subjective, then you're free to create your own reality, whether that reality is good or bad.

☑ Takeover Rule #1: ☑

***If you accept the idea that you create your own
reality, then you can change it!***

Changing our reality is not an easy thing to do. Most of us are very protective of our beliefs, values, biases, and interpretations of reality. In my leadership seminars, I often have participants who come from out of town and stay at the hotel where the seminar is being held. When they check in, each of them brings their luggage that holds all of their clothes and other stuff they think they'll need to get through the week. They probably have toiletries, shirts or blouses, slacks or skirts—and a bathing suit if they are true optimists.

Imagine you're one of these seminar attendees. Imagine further that, as you stand at the front desk checking into the hotel, a man walks up and begins eyeing your suitcase. Then, suddenly, this man begins walking around your suitcase, looking at it, kicking it a little bit, and touching it. What would go through your mind? Would you wonder what this lunatic was doing? Would you eye him suspiciously?

Now assume this man becomes more serious about your suitcase and begins clawing at it. You probably will, in turn, become more serious about protecting it. If he were to try to open it, you would probably grab it and wrench it from his hands, yelling something like, "Get away from my stuff, you jerk!"

We do the same thing with our beliefs, values, and biases—in other words, our personal realities. We are very protective of the things we hold near and dear. We don't like people messing with our beliefs. Yet, these very beliefs may be hampering our future and getting in the way of personal improvement.

Our view of reality can either work against us or for us. We are often so protective of our view, so bent on keeping it away from the intrusions of others, that we never have a chance to see if maybe the beliefs we carry are dragging us down and holding us back, instead of moving us ahead.

☑ Takeover Rule #2: ☑

***Your view of reality can either
work against you or for you.***

We often support our picture of reality by discounting any of the information we don't want to see. Wade and Ann work for an advertising agency. They started at about the same time and are in roughly similar positions in the creative department. Wade and Ann see one another as competition. In fact, they disagree regularly on the best approach to advertising campaigns. Wade is suspicious of Ann, and she is suspicious of him. Each has a view of the other as being in it for only him- or herself and being willing to do anything necessary to get ahead at the expense of everybody else. Wade is very wary of Ann's motives. As a result of his view of her, Wade will filter information, so that any time Ann does something that supports his view of her as ill-intentioned, it becomes another black mark against her on his mental ledger and further convinces him she is not trustworthy.

☑ Takeover Rule #3: ☑

Create a more flexible view of reality by not discounting information you don't want to see.

Let's say Ann does something really good and kindhearted. For instance, she gives Wade credit for a concept that turned into a very successful ad campaign. What will be Wade's response? Will he say that Ann is not such a bad person and is obviously trying to improve the relationship?

In fact, what often happens is just the opposite. A person in Wade's situation will often discount Ann's behavior, because he believes her underlying intent is malicious even though on the surface it may be positive. As a result, he filters out any situations and examples of behavior that contrast with his negative view of Ann, so that when she gives him credit for the advertising campaign, he looks for ulterior motives. He decides that Ann has given him credit because she suspects that the campaign will bomb after its initial success and wants to make sure that everyone knows that Wade was responsible for the catastrophe. Any indication of Ann as an upright, honorable coworker is discounted to keep her in the box Wade has created in his mind for her.

Scenario

This same kind of filtering can happen on a much larger scale. Ralph is engaged in a conversation with his friend, Farid.

"Farid, I can't believe what I read recently about that Gallup poll."

"What Gallup poll?"

"You know, the one where they interviewed people in nine Muslim countries, and something like 61 percent of the people didn't believe Arabs were responsible for the World Trade Center attack."

"Well, I don't believe they did it, either."

"What? Are you nuts? They've got pictures of the guys."

"Come on, Ralph. Those pictures don't prove anything. It's just like that O.J. Simpson trial. The guy was found not guilty by the jury, yet a lot of you guys still think he's guilty."

"Well, he *is* guilty!"

Both Ralph and Farid have chosen to hold on to a belief even if many others view an incident quite differently. In the World Trade Center attack, Americans believe quite firmly that Muslims were responsible, yet many Muslims disagree. In the case of O.J. Simpson, many African Americans believe he was innocent, yet many Caucasian Americans feel just the opposite.

We all apply this type of filter to support our views or beliefs. If we understand this filtering process, we can begin letting in the data that conflicts with our present view. This is not easy. We often see others who hold different views as naive. But if we accept that reality is subjective and that our view may be wrong, we open ourselves up to new approaches that can move our lives forward more productively. By doing this, we increase our potential for achieving success and a true sense of well-being.

Find your own example of a misperceived reality

To determine if you have ever been guilty of misperceiving reality—and were, therefore, setting up roadblocks to a personal takeover—do the following exercise:

1.   Think back and identify a belief that at one point in your life you were certain was true and later discovered was not. It can be work or career related (for example, being certain your boss will never give you a promotion). It also can involve other areas of life, such as a certainty that you'd never receive an "A" in a given course, a conviction that attractive men or women never date less attractive men or women, a certainty that the Soviet Union will always be a communist country, etc. Write down this belief.

2.   Identify the reasons you were so certain this reality was absolute and permanent at the time. Specifically:

   •   Was it because you took one incident or fact and made a false assumption based on incomplete evidence?

   •   Was it because others you admired told you something was true or confirmed your belief?

   •   Was it because you were fixated on certain facts and ignored or discounted others that would have changed your view of reality?

   •   Was it because you used twisted logic and rationalization to convince yourself of your reality?

3.   With the benefit of hindsight, note how your misperceived reality affected you at the time. Specifically:

   •   Did it prevent you from taking advantage of a job or career opportunity?

   •   Did it hurt your job or career in any other way?

   •   Did it alienate other people who perceived this reality differently?

   •   Did it cause you to be strident and irrational or harm any valued relationships?

When you start the process of launching a personal take-over, you should keep this exercise in mind. It will help you recognize that reality is flexible and that you needn't be bound by what seem to be inflexible rules, facts, or constraints. As you'll soon discover, what you think or believe doesn't stay in your head but directly translates to what you do. That's why people who have mastered personal takeovers are acutely aware of how their thoughts impact their actions.

Chapter 2

The Impact of Our Beliefs

❝ *I thought you were in Mensa,*
until you spelled it wrong.❞

PERSONAL TAKEOVERS DEMAND BOTH A HEALTHY OUTER AND inner view. You not only need to understand your own perception of reality in the ways just discussed, but you must learn to develop a mindset that puts you, rather than others, in charge of your life. Unfortunately, many of us have developed mindsets where we've ceded power to others. We fail to realize that our most significant battles are waged within ourselves; that we need to conquer our own fears if we're going to be happy and successful. Instead, we engage in battles with others, believing that if we're going to be happy and successful, we need to conquer a competitor or convince a boss of our worth.

You can't launch a personal takeover if you're operating with too many liabilities. If you're burdened with mindset debt—if you feel you owe your success to others or you're convinced that you'll never achieve certain goals because you lack the contacts or talent—you can never perform a full takeover for yourself. One of the best ways to eliminate this debt is by becoming aware of the common ways this debt is incurred. Let's look at how we form personal beliefs that keep us stuck in our ruts.

The birth of belief: Why we believe what we do and how it can hold us back

In the field of mathematics, axioms are fundamental truths or principles about mathematical relationships. We each have mindsets about life that are as absolute to us as these axioms are to mathematics. These *mindsets* are our most fundamental beliefs about ourselves, others, work, family, friends, and virtually every other aspect of life.

Consider, however, what might happen if some of these axioms are incorrect. What if a given belief that you've held for years turned out to be fatally flawed in some way? Many of us harbor such beliefs. We've held them for so long and so hard, they seem like they must be true. That's because they often form as a result of the earliest messages we received from our parents, our first teachers, and from kids in the neighborhood. These beliefs harden into mindsets, and whether accurate or not, they're difficult to doubt.

Perhaps your parents told you that you couldn't be trusted, or perhaps your parents gave you signals that you were an unwanted child. What if they told you that you were not dependable? I've seen many adults who have the belief that they can't do anything right, a belief that often began as a result of messages from their parents.

A lot of messages are delivered to us as we are growing up, from our earliest days in school. An experience with my son shows how this happens. Tommy was having significant problems in his third grade English class. The problems grew, culminating in a meeting between myself, Tommy, and the teacher. The teacher began the meeting, and for a solid 45 minutes talked about all of the things that Tommy had done wrong, how poor he was as a student, and how unlikely it would be for him to improve. During the entire time, not one positive comment was made about Tommy's abilities or behaviors.

As Tommy and I sat listening to the teacher, she stopped abruptly and said, "Let me give you an example of what I mean." She turned to Tommy and said, "Tommy, tell me what a noun is." Without hesitating, Tommy responded, "A person, place, or thing." Now my reaction was to be very proud, thinking to myself that Tommy does know his English, but my pride was quickly dashed. The teacher turned to me and said, "See, he doesn't understand what a noun is." I was puzzled. "What do you mean?" I asked. "Well, Dr. Gabel," she responded, "everybody knows that a noun is the *name* of a person, place, or thing."

Think of the impact in later work life on the individual who regularly receives the message that he or she is incompetent. These messages contribute to developing our mindsets. They are like a computer program that runs in each of us. In some cases, the mindsets are positive and really work for us. In other cases, they are negative and work against us. But in each case, they are almost indelibly imprinted.

We establish rules of behavior as a result of these mindsets. We might call these rules of behavior *defenses*. Defenses guide our daily actions, and are based on our mindsets. These defenses are there to protect us.

Accompanying these defenses is the *self-talk* that goes on continually in our head. This self-talk goes on whenever we meet somebody new, whenever an incident occurs, or just in our daily experience. Some researchers call it the script that goes on within our minds—a script that keeps reaffirming our mindsets. The following example illustrates how all this works.

Scenario

Jason is counseling his fellow worker, Manuel.

"Manuel, what's that I saw you doing yesterday?"

"I was supervising the guys unloading those boxcars."

"You're not a supervisor."

"I know, but Joey's on vacation. And Martin asked me if

I wanted to try my hand at this. No promises, but he said if I did a good job, he'd put my name in for the next team leader job."

"Man, you're a sap. Don't you know you can't trust management? Martin just wants you to do this so he can take advantage of you."

"Take advantage? How?"

"Is he paying you extra to do this?"

"Well, no."

"You never, never take on additional responsibilities like this unless they pay you for them first!"

Jason has a *mindset* that management cannot be trusted and will take advantage of workers. Workers who distrust management often set a *defense* that they will not assume any additional work responsibilities unless they are paid for these tasks in advance. Why would that be? If I believe that management may take advantage of me, then I can never let them get the upper hand. When Jason saw Manuel taking on the extra work, Jason's mind started racing with *self-talk*, "Oh boy, they're using Manuel," or "These guys think they can get away with anything."

What do you think Manuel's boss's response would be if he were to tell him, "I'm not going to take this position without additional pay immediately"? If he is like many people, he will respond with something like, "Suit yourself. I'll find someone who is willing to take that risk." The opportunity that might have been available to Manuel would disappear, and it was the defense suggested by Jason that caused him to decline the opportunity.

Now I'll give you a chance to see how your beliefs influence your response to a specific situation. If you are employed now, imagine that you are performing the job you currently hold. If you don't currently work, imagine that you're employed by an organization in a capacity appropriate to your experience and skills. As you read the situation, try to put yourself into it. Act as if this were really happening to you.

The situation

Your company has hired a new CEO. The company has not been profitable, so this CEO has been brought in to turn the situation around. She has a reputation as a real hatchet-woman and announces that there is immediately going to be a 25 percent reduction in staff. All areas will be affected equally.

In the area below, write down whatever thoughts come to mind. These might be thoughts about the new CEO, the company, what will happen to you, or any other thoughts that flow through your mind.

My Thoughts (My Self-Talk)

_____

_____

_____

_____

_____

What did you write? Did you think, *Surely, I'm going to be the one losing my job*, or *They wouldn't let me go because I'm too valuable*? Was the message to yourself that you are a very valuable employee, or did you, instead, think that you are expendable? What thoughts did you have about the company? Did you think, *They're not going to do this fairly,* or did you believe that they would somehow cheat you out of your position?

Our self-talk offers an insight into the mindsets we hold. For instance, if you had thought, *They're not going to do this fairly*, it might indicate that you have a cynical mindset about how companies operate. Perhaps your belief or mindset in this situation might be *Companies cannot be trusted to do the right thing*.

Was your self-talk optimistic, skeptical, sarcastic, self-deprecating, ambitious? Take a minute to write below some of your mindsets relative to work and about yourself, thinking of the situation identified above. Strive to identify both positive and negative thoughts about work and about your own abilities.

My Mindsets About Work

_____

_____

_____

_____

_____

Were the positive mindsets you wrote about work and about your own abilities easy to find, or did you struggle? How about the negative ones? One mindset that pops up surprisingly often is, *I'm not very good*. I've found many people who could be quite successful but have a belief that they are not very good and have a shallow view of their skills and abilities. A pervasive thought many hold is, *When others find out about me, they'll see that I miss important things on the job*. What are your beliefs or mindsets about others in your company? Do you feel you can't trust them, that they wouldn't take the time to make a reasonable judgment about you?

Now that you've identified some of your mindsets, write any defenses that you have established for yourself as a result of the more negative ones.

Defenses

_____

_____

_____

_____

_____

Some of us set a defense of not staying too long at any one job. That might be a negative defense, in that it keeps us moving to other jobs instead of gaining mastery in one. Some defenses, however, might be very positive for us. One such defense is to educate ourselves continually so we are ready to find another position should our employer let us go.

Mindsets have consequences. What you believe is intimately connected with what you do, even though it may be an unconscious connection. It's very difficult for people with cynical, pessimistic, or paranoid mindsets to achieve great things. They may want to achieve great things, but their belief that people are conspiring against their success (for instance) will limit their actions; they won't trust enough people to make the alliances necessary to achieve their goals.

Our mindsets and defenses cause us to establish certain relationships with a given group of people while avoiding relationships with others. If we are more distrustful of people, we will end up having few relationships, and those we do have will lack the openness and intimacy necessary for mutually beneficial partnerships. On the other hand, when our mindsets are optimistic and positive, we are much more willing to form relationships with a wide variety of people and extend trust to them. This facilitates networking, building alliances with others, and just plain teamwork—all critical skills in today's environment.

To understand how our mindsets determine the type of people with whom we surround ourselves, consider teenagers. Academically accomplished teenagers often pal around with people very similar to themselves. This becomes their reference group—a group that values education and likes to talk about it. On the other hand, teenagers who believe school is a waste of time, do as little as possible, and receive poor grades tend to form relationships with adolescents who share these traits.

Jobs also represent our mindsets. The type of job we take represents our belief about our own abilities. It also often represents our predisposition toward risk. Some people will accept whatever job comes along because they feel they can't handle a more demanding job. Some of us are terrified of jumping on a big opportunity in another state, because we question our ability to grasp the new job quickly enough and are fearful we'd be stuck far from home.

At the end of my senior year at Cooley High School in Detroit, the French teacher, Miss Bodzin, pulled her students together. We had each taken four years of high school French. Miss Bodzin informed us that we could apply to the Sorbonne in Paris for our university studies, because we each had a decent command of the French language. I immediately dismissed the possibility. There was no way I was going to go to another country. My limiting mindset prevented me from exploring an opportunity that might have been marvelous for my personal development.

The mindsets you hold are an important part of your entire being. It is important to recognize their value, because they provide an internal support structure for you. Your beliefs are responsible for what you've achieved in your career (or what you haven't achieved). They have also seen you through many tough times, times when you felt you could depend on no one but yourself.

Scenario

Kaitlin is a senior in college and works full time in a music store. She prides herself on her aggressiveness. She is talking to a fellow employee at the cash register.

"Look, no one is going to take advantage of me. I see too many people who get walked over because they're afraid to stand up for themselves. I just got a paper back last week in Economics with a 'B' grade. I marched right over to the professor's office and got in his face. I told him this was an 'A' paper. He began to debate me, but I countered everything he said. He finally backed down and gave me an 'A-.' Better than a 'B,' huh?"

A customer walks up and informs Kaitlin that she has a CD she wants to return.

"Let's see it," says Kaitlin. The customer hands over the CD, and Kaitlin gives it a cursory glance. "Why are you returning it?"

"It doesn't play right."

Kaitlin turns it over several times, examining it for scratches. "Looks like you've played this a couple thousand times. We're not gonna take it back."

"But don't you have a store policy of giving refunds with no questions asked?"

"Listen, that applies to items still in their packages. You've used this, and now you want to return it. Well, I'm not going to do it. If you want to buy a replacement CD, they're on sale right now. But that's all we'll do for you."

The customer grabs the CD, throws it back in her bag, and hurries out of the store.

"See? If I didn't challenge her, she would have been given a refund on that worthless CD. If you let them, people will take advantage of you. I don't let them."

Kaitlin takes an aggressive approach toward people because she believes if she doesn't, people will take advantage of her. So, if we think about the concept of mindsets, a significant mindset Kaitlin holds is, *People will try to take advantage of me,* and a defense she has created is, *To prevent them taking advantage, I must be more aggressive than them.* In some ways, Kaitlin is correct. Her aggressive approach broadcasts a message to those around her that she will not be bullied. Of course, what Kaitlin isn't seeing is the downside of her particular mindset and resulting defense. Her mindset will actually prevent Kaitlin from creating relationships with all but the most tolerant people. She is never going to be the manager of the record store because her suspicious nature would alienate most direct-reports.

It's amazing how oblivious we are to how our beliefs hold us back. In the previous example, Kaitlin believes that her combination of hard work, aggressive behavior, and untrusting attitude is helping her do well in her chosen field, but she fails to see how her mindset has placed limits on this success. A discussion with the Regional Manager for the CD chain where Kaitlin works demonstrates this.

"Kaitlin's been with us for three years. She is a hard worker, and she's smart. But, I have had more complaints about her than all of the other employees put together. She came up to me last time I was in the store and said she wants to be a store manager. I said I'd think about it. If I had been honest with her, I would have told her I can't promote her. We'd lose the staff. She'd tell every one of them off. I've only kept her because she's such a hard worker. If I could only keep her away from customers...."

In light of the example with Kaitlin, keep the following truism in mind:

☑ Takeover Rule #4: ☑

Your mindsets have gotten you where you are today.
They have also kept you where you are today.

The thoughts you have right now are emanating from your mindsets. They are causing you to behave in certain ways, just like we have seen with Kaitlin. People often believe that what they do will determine their future. This is true, but they fail to realize that what they do is predicated on what they believe. Time and again, I've seen people try and fail to change their behaviors. They've received negative comments in performance reviews and vow to change their ways. Unfortunately, they have great difficulty changing their behaviors because they've avoided changing their beliefs. The good news is that it's entirely possible to change your thoughts and thereby change your future for the better.

Actions versus beliefs: The takeover challenge

Personal takeovers pose a particular challenge for those who focus on changing actions to the exclusion of beliefs. Many times, these people have achieved things in life by taking action, and they figure that personal takeovers are simply a matter of following the prescribed steps. In reality, you can follow these steps and fail to achieve a takeover because you haven't changed your beliefs. If in the back of your mind you're convinced that your future is primarily determined by chance or you are skeptical that others view you in a positive light, you're going to be undermined by these beliefs. On the surface, you may do what is necessary for a personal takeover, but beneath the surface your thoughts will sabotage your efforts.

We can often see this dichotomy between action and belief occur when a person receives negative feedback during a performance review. The supervisor informs the employee that he or she must behave differently if they wish to receive a higher rating in the future. The employee agrees to the behavior, but doesn't really believe the supervisor.

The following discussion shows how this dialogue might progress.

"Chelsea, the reason your performance has been rated unsatisfactory, and you have been given no pay increase, is due to the fact that you have consistently had major run-ins with customers of the bank."

"I don't know of any major run-ins."

"Well, how about when Mr. Daniels from the American Cancer Society came up to your window and you asked him for a cigarette?"

I hate these do-gooders, trying to get all of us to kick the habit. I'm glad he never told them about the time I blew smoke right into his face when I ran into him outside the bank. "That was all a misunderstanding. I apologized to him."

"Yeah, after you told him more people get cancer from x-rays than from cigarettes. And how about the customer from the Nature Conservancy who complained that you told him how you like to change the oil in your car and take the old oil and dump it in the woods?"

That was a hoot. He was mortified when I told him that. Boy, living in California was the wrong choice for me. I should have stayed in Jersey. These people are such pansies. "Listen, another misunderstanding. I think he just overreacted."

"Well, overreact or not, Chelsea, I can't allow you to talk to customers this way. We have many environmentally and socially conscious customers. They deserve better treatment. I expect you to refrain from these disruptive statements and behaviors."

You have no sense of humor, and these customers are way too sensitive. "Okay, I hear you. I will do my best to behave with these customers." *I have to figure a way to be a little more subtle in the way I insult these jerks.*

As you can probably guess, the prognosis is not good for Chelsea's change of behavior. She doesn't really see the need to change. She doesn't feel remorse about what she has done. She'll possibly make a half-hearted attempt to change her behavior because her boss has imposed consequences on her; however, changes of behavior without the necessary changes in belief are typically short-lived.

As we see in Chelsea's case, she is not really committed to changing her behavior. She is doing it in an attempt to survive on the job. Her basic beliefs, however, have not changed. As long as Chelsea holds on to these thoughts about certain groups and believes in her heart that her behavior is okay, nothing long term can change. Even if Chelsea does want to keep her job and agrees that she shouldn't behave in the same way as she has toward these philanthropic groups, her behavior is still at odds with her beliefs.

While the whole idea of changing one's beliefs may seem quite hard to do, at the same time there is an enormous personal power that comes to the individual who realizes the secret of Takeover Rule #5. Simply put, if I want to change my future I can do it. I merely have to change the thoughts that are dominating my mind. I can build an entirely new future for myself if I am willing to shift my own mindset. This will result in the corollary behavior change that attends a change in mindset. Then both my behavior and my beliefs are in sync with one another.

☑ Takeover Rule #5: ☑

The thoughts you have right now determine your future. You can change your future by merely changing your thoughts.

The following "What If…" exercise is designed to help you identify how your beliefs might help or hinder your takeover actions:

Some of the scenarios below may make you feel uncomfortable and you may be tempted to provide what you believe
is the right answer rather than the one that represents your true
self in a given situation. Though this impulse is understandable, resist it and describe exactly what you would think and
do if the following circumstances existed:

1.   What if you had the chance to be promoted to your
      "dream job" within your organization? Do you believe
      you would be capable of handling this position? Do
      any doubts come to mind about your ability to handle
      this job? If you were given this dream job, what might
      happen to turn the job into a nightmare? When your
      dreams have come true in the past, have they turned
      out to be less than you dreamed?

2.   What if the future of your company and all its employees
      rested in your hands? Do you believe you would be
      capable of meeting this challenge? What would you
      think to yourself if the CEO said to you, "I'm placing
      the fate of this company in your hands?" Would you
      be excited about the challenge and confident about your
      abilities? Or would you make a sarcastic remark to
      yourself like, *The CEO has just chosen the absolute
      worst person for the job.*

3.   What if you were given an opportunity of a lifetime—
      a chance to run your own company, a terrific job, a
      posting to an office in Hawaii—but the opportunity
      was tied to working with someone you crossed swords
      with in the past? Would you immediately say to your-
      self, *This is a great opportunity, but it's too bad it will
      never work because I can't stand that person.* Or would
      you take the view, *The opportunity is so good that I'll
      find a way to make this relationship work.*

4.   What if you were stranded on a desert island with a
      carton containing all the parts and tools necessary to

build a boat? Let's further assume that you've never built a boat before and don't have a high degree of mechanical aptitude. And let's further assume you open the crate, start trying to build the boat and become frustrated by its complexity. Would you believe you were totally incapable of completing this task? Would you curse the fates that stranded you on the island and failed to bless you with mechanical aptitude? Or would you doggedly pursue the task, believing that given time (of which you have plenty) and persistence, you'll manage to fashion a seaworthy vessel?

Reflect on the theme that runs through your answers to these four questions. Were you consistently optimistic or pessimistic? Did you question or have faith in your abilities? What do your answers tell you about the mindsets you have about your own abilities and work? Have you set up any defenses because of these mindsets? Did your self-talk reflect a willingness to try or an unwillingness to attempt the "impossible"?

The odds are that you were at least somewhat skeptical and pessimistic. Most of us are, which is why we don't naturally perform personal takeovers. Adjusting your beliefs, however, will enable you to build a boat and escape from the metaphorical island on which you've stranded yourself.

Chapter 3

Jumping Through Hoops

> " *If I knew life was this tough,*
> *I wouldn't have shaved my legs."*

WHEN I WAS A YOUNG BOY, MY MOTHER TOOK ME TO THE circus. One of the acts at the circus was a man who had five dogs. They each looked to be about the size of a Chihuahua. He had a number of hoops and began his act by holding one hoop up in the air about a foot off the ground. Each of the dogs proceeded to jump through the hoop. After they had all jumped through the first hoop, he made it a little harder. He held the hoop about two feet off the ground, and the dogs proceeded to jump through the hoop again, to the delight of the audience who would yelp themselves as they saw these little dogs straining to reach the higher hoop.

The act continued until the dogs were now jumping through a series of hoops, at all angles, and were running around in circles. One particularly tiny dog had to work like the dickens to get through the hoops. Near the end of the act, when the hoops were being held high off the ground, the littlest dog would literally jump up and hang on the hoop as it attempted to squirm and pull itself through. It got to the point where I felt sorry for the poor dogs, on their endless run in circles, trying to please their master.

Some of us seem to experience something akin to those circus dogs. We only see ourselves through the eyes of others. We find ourselves continually jumping through hoops, trying to please them. We read things into their facial gestures, sure that they are displeased even though we only glimpse the hint of a frown. We attempt to read our success in their faces, instead of looking within ourselves to determine if *we* feel successful.

Jumping through hoops occurs as a result of an unproductive, counter takeover mindset that says your self worth can only be determined through other people's eyes. Unfortunately, many of us cling to this mindset in uncertain times, convinced that we can only be successful if our boss (or a customer, client, or some other person of importance to us) approves of our ideas and actions. The problem, of course, is that you can't complete a takeover when you view things this way, because you've essentially "sold" yourself to another owner. When you jump through hoops, you've given up control, as the following example illustrates.

How high can you jump?

Scenario

Troy, a young manager in a mid-sized packaged goods company, was talking with Luis, another manager in his group, about a report that he had just turned in to his boss.

"I gave Sherry the report. I can tell she's not happy with it. She responded with a grunt and a look of disgust when I handed it to her."

"Are you sure that was directed at you?" Luis said.

"Who else would it be directed at? I don't think she likes me. She never goes out of her way to say anything nice."

"Troy, she's never said anything negative about you or your work. She's just a very animated person."

At that moment, Sherry walked out of her office. "Hey Troy, this doesn't look bad," she said with a smile, holding up his report, and returned to her office.

"See, now, don't you think you were overreacting before?" Luis asked.

"Yeah, I guess I was. Whew, I feel a lot better. I guess I should relax a little and not react to every facial mannerism I see."

"You'd be a lot better off that way," said Luis.

The door of Sherry's office opened again and she stepped out. "Luis, I'd like you to present this report that Troy put together tomorrow at the committee meeting. Troy, I'm going to have Luis do it because he has more experience with the Management Committee meetings, and I won't be there." She returned to her office.

"See, Luis, what did I tell you? She has no confidence in me."

Troy is jumping through hoops. His emotions are riding a roller coaster, rising with the hint of positive vibes from Sherry and plunging whenever anything she says could be construed as the least bit negative. Interestingly enough, Sherry isn't even the one holding the hoops. Troy is creating them in his mind, trying to read messages in her words, her tone of voice, words left unspoken, and even her body language.

When we behave in this manner, we create as many issues for those around us as for ourselves. For instance, Luis must sometimes console Troy, but challenge him at other times because of his inaccurate perceptions of events. Troy becomes, in Luis's eyes, a "high maintenance" person. He can expect Troy to approach him regularly, displaying a beaten-down look, desperate for Luis's support. This results in endless hours of discussion each month as Luis must try to help Troy see that he is reading too much into events, messages, or the looks of others.

Troy also becomes high maintenance for his boss, Sherry. He will react to everything she says, to every action she takes. If she gives an assignment to someone other than Troy, he will be convinced it's because she didn't like him, trust him, or have confidence in him. His mood swings will likely hinge on things she says or does, and at some point she'll notice his overreactions. At this point, she may actually lose some trust in him because of his inappropriate responses.

The person who suffers the greatest consequences from Troy's perception of things is Troy himself. His life is miserable as he attempts to read subliminal messages into the actions and statements of others. He continually judges himself based on whether he believes others accept him or not. The hoops are endless for Troy, and he will never be able to achieve a takeover until he stops basing his feelings of success and achievement on other people's reactions to what he does.

This tendency to jump through hoops is often a conditioned response. From the time we were little, some of us have been "trained" to seek approbation from parents, teachers, mentors, and bosses. It is an unthinking reflex rather than a rational way of dealing with issues in our lives. You can see how irrational and reflexive this response is when you view it through the lens of personal relationships.

Scenario

Marybeth is waiting to be picked up for a date with her boyfriend, Shane.

I wish he would hurry up. I can't stand to be away from him. I feel so much better when I'm around him.

The doorbell rings, and Marybeth goes down to answer it. It's Shane.

"Hi, Marybeth," he begins. "Where would you like to go for dinner?"

"Anywhere you'd like sounds great," she replies.

I want him to know that he's the focus for me—that I'm happy no matter where we are.

"You never choose a place Marybeth. Don't you have any opinions of your own?"

Oh no! He's unhappy with me. I've got to show him I'm assertive. "Well, how about Villa Maria?"

"That sounds good. They have great food."

Wonderful. He thinks I have good taste in restaurants.

"Just one thing, uhh, Marybeth. I don't have any money. Can you buy tonight? I'll owe you one."

I should have shown him I was more sensitive. Poor guy, he's been out of work for three years. And I like the way he stands up for his principles, that a guy with a GED shouldn't have to take a job for less than 40 thousand dollars a year. I want to make sure he knows I'm generous. Plus, going to Villa Maria will stretch out the evening.

"Sure, I'd be happy to pay. And why don't I drive?"

This way I've got him in my car. He always seems to leave right after dinner. Yet, he's never home. I go nuts when I feel so out of control like this. I just feel less of a person when I'm not with him. I feel so fortunate to have met him.

There are, unfortunately, a lot of Marybeths among us. They jump through hoops at work, and they jump through hoops in relationships. They are always attempting to interpret what someone else is wanting from them, rather than just being themselves or doing what they believe to be the right thing. Their lives turn into an endless quagmire of twists and turns, as they try to be something they aren't and jump through the hoops that become more and more difficult over time. When they attempt to live and work this way, they end up on this emotional roller coaster.

I am not advocating that you ignore others' opinions. If your manager is displeased with something you say or do, you should try and understand her point of view. There is nothing wrong with wanting people in the organization (and outside of it) to like you. This is natural. When conflicts arise, you should attempt to resolve the issue and get the relationship back on an even keel. Takeover thinkers fully believe themselves capable of resolving conflicts and managing relationships, no matter how powerful or important the other person in the relationship is. They realize they have tremendous personal power that has nothing to do with position or money. Don't act like Jeremy, in the following situation, under the mistaken belief that you're exhibiting takeover thinking.

Jeremy is a professor in the School of Business Administration at an Eastern university. He believes it is his right to do whatever he pleases—period. Let's listen as he talks about his view of the world.

"People would like to control me or make me conform to their ways, but they can't," begins Jeremy. "I'll do whatever I want. The university came out last week with a sort of policy where they encourage us to wear business attire, so that we can create some sort of image for the students. I decided their rule was stupid, so all last week I came to work in light cotton slacks and a sweatshirt with sandals and no socks. Well, the Dean was obviously nervous about saying anything to me. So, he avoided me. I made sure to parade myself in front of his office so he'd have to see me challenging their stupid idea.

"They encourage us to have regular office hours for the students. If I meet with students, I don't have time to do research, so I meet with them as little as possible. They take up a lot of time with all their questions, and I can't believe how many want to convince me I graded something wrong. I don't have time for that, and I don't hesitate to tell them so. I've had some complaints, but the university isn't going to do anything, so let them complain.

"The Dean came to me a few weeks back and said he wanted to reorganize the department, and since we're all a team, he'd like me to be involved. I said, 'No thanks. Let me know how things turn out.' He was furious with me, but he can't do anything to me since I have tenure."

When you embark upon a personal takeover, you're not disregarding others' views or opinions the way Jeremy has. Instead, you're shifting your focus toward what's the right choice for you to make, considering your personal values and beliefs.

There will always be someone out there who is not going to like you for reasons known only to him. No matter what action you take or decision you make, someone will criticize you for that action or that decision. If you can accept this criticism as a given, then you're free to choose actions and decisions because they represent your values and your beliefs. You fully believe these are powerful values and beliefs and that they can withstand whatever criticism is leveled at them. Takeover thinkers accept that they can't please everyone, which leads us to Takeover Rule #6.

☑ Takeover Rule #6: ☑

You can never make everyone happy. Choose the actions that are right for you, accepting that there will always be someone ready to criticize you.

To determine if you are jumping through hoops, answer the following questions:

1. Do I judge my own success by what other people think of me?

2. Do I find that I have significant mood swings and remain stuck in a mood for a sustained period of time after a positive or negative remark?

3. Do I focus a lot on whether or not someone likes me?

4. Do I spend a lot of time talking with others about somebody's body language or actions and how those reflect their opinion of me?

5. Do I find myself depressed or ecstatic based on what my boss, mentor, or major customer/client says about me?

6. Do I find myself locked into a career path that is a mirror image of the one carved by my boss or mentor?

7. Do I spend many sleepless nights and waste many office hours replaying a negative comment that someone at work made to me?

8. Do I have career goals that bear little relation to my own personal interests, requirements, and beliefs?

If you find yourself answering yes to some or all of these questions, recognize that you're jumping through hoops. To stop yourself from doing so—and to facilitate your personal takeover—keep the following points in mind:

- You cannot control other people's opinions of you, no matter what you do or how hard you try.

- People come to conclusions about you based less on your actions than on their own values, biases, and beliefs.

- When people react negatively to something you do or say, they sometimes are reacting more to their own sense of insecurity than anything else.

- You can waste incredible amounts of time trying to decipher other people's statements and actions without gaining anything from the effort.

A personal takeover, on the other hand, is your acknowledgement that you can only be yourself and attempt to do the right thing. Sometimes others will agree with your action or decision, and sometimes they won't. It is pointless to spend precious hours of your life trying to decipher every statement made or action taken by others.

Conditionally defining our success

A form of jumping through hoops is particularly insidious in keeping us from launching successful takeovers. It's called conditional well-being. Instead of jumping through hoops based on other people's reactions to us, we jump through hoops based on our misguided notions of success and happiness. Instead of striving to achieve our deeply personal visions and goals, we attempt to achieve illusory goals. By illusory, I mean that they're based on the norms of a particular group or the media; they're what everyone in our social group defines as success, or they're how everyone we play golf with describes happiness. So our success and happiness is tied to some condition over which we have no control.

For instance, you feel you really haven't "made it" until you buy a home in a highly desirable community (a location condition). Or you haven't really succeeded until you are earning a certain salary (a money condition). Or you're not truly happy until you've been accepted into an exclusive club (a social condition).

For most of us, this conditional sense of well-being starts when we're young. We receive all As and a B but we don't consider that successful because our parents ask us, "Why wasn't that B an A?" Or we envy the most popular kid in school and we can't be happy because we're not that popular. Success and happiness, therefore, become conditional. When this happens, we can't take control of our lives because we believe success and happiness reside in certain group norms.

The following conversation between Michael and Jake reflects conditional thinking.

"Hey, Jake, want another beer?"

"Sure, why not?"

"Well, I just got that new 45-foot Sea Ray I was telling you about."

"Mike, we live in Arizona. Where are you going to dock that thing?"

"Well, when I became a VP, the President had me over for dinner and told me about his cruiser down in Anguilla. Thought I might get a place down there after I marry Donna."

"Donna? You mean that woman who is so vicious and mean-spirited, they said she belongs in Human Resources?"

"Yeah, but she's so beautiful. If she would only marry me, my life would be set."

"Didn't you say that when you married your third wife, Julie?"

"Yeah, but this one's different...."

Mike's happiness and success is contingent on things outside of himself—on purchasing a specific type of boat or on marrying the most beautiful woman. Because his boss has a Sea Ray, he feels he has to have one. Mike actually believes that his "life would be set" if a mean and vicious, but beautiful woman would marry him. Mike will never take full control of his life until he realizes that he is letting other people define that life.

Think about the three ways people usually define success. For some of us, success is a purely materialistic concept. We won't consider ourselves successful until we are able to buy a home in a certain type of community, purchase a certain type of car, or make a specific amount of money. We have let advertising or a peer group or some other outside source dictate the terms of our success from a purely materialistic standpoint.

Another definition of success involves fame. The cult of celebrity is pervasive in our society, and we dream of being on the covers of *People* or *Fortune* magazines; of being famous actors, sports stars, or politicians; of becoming a household name. If we fall short of this elusive goal, we feel our life hasn't measured up. We think our life is dull in comparison with famous people, no matter what we achieve on our own terms.

Others define success from a relationship perspective. They believe they will never be "whole" unless they marry someone like Donna. You probably know people who fall in love at the drop of a hat and who are completely and utterly miserable until they enter into a relationship. And then the relationship sours, they break up, and the whole cycle begins again. Their belief is that they can't make themselves happy, that they need someone else to make them happy.

There's nothing wrong with wanting fame, fortune, and relationships; they're all good things. But they become bad things when we make our happiness and success completely contingent upon their acquisition. Whenever we live by the doctrine of conditional well-being, we've given our power away.

How do you define success? Make a check mark next to the statement or statements that you feel best represent what's important to you:

1.   I dream about the day when I'm well-known by people.
2.   I am searching for just the right person to complete my life; until I find that person, I am not whole.

3. When I fantasize about my future, I usually think about being talked about in admiring terms by friends and coworkers.

4. What drives me is a desire to show people in my past that they were wrong about me; they said I would never be a success, and I'm going to show them they were wrong.

5. I know I'll have made it when I can afford to build a home with a three-car garage in _____ (prestigious location).

6. All I want is a six-figure salary.

7. Since I was in school, I've been eyeing a capstone position in this industry; I'm never going to consider myself a success unless I get that position.

8. I'm never going to be happy until I'm doing as well as _____ (person who you know, grew up with, or work with).

If you didn't check any of the above statements, congratulations! The odds are, your definition of success is not contingent on external things or people. If you did check one or more, you're probably in the majority of readers. The following letters represent the three common definitions of success: M—material things, F—fame, R—relationships. Here is the "key" for the eight questions listed: 1) F, 2) R, 3) F, 4) R, 5) M, 6) M, 7) F, 8) R.

Do you see a pattern in your responses? If so, you have a good sense of your definition of success and the specific ways in which you have ceded control of it to others. This awareness will come in handy as you begin your personal takeover.

The comparison trap

In an affluent society, the grass is always greener in the other person's yard. Just 50 years ago, most people were raised in relatively small apartments or houses; the majority of Baby

Boomers started out life in a house that had less than 1,000 square feet of space. Today, some people don't consider themselves successful if they are living in any house under 2,000 square feet. And in many upscale communities, the norm is 4,000 or more. Why? Is this because we derive more intrinsic pleasure from a bigfoot home? For some, it's merely the ability to make the statement "I live in this huge space because I can," with the secret hope that others will acknowledge how successful we are.

This same conditional idea of success is seen in people joining country clubs for the prestige involved, marrying into money, acquiring "arm candy," or starving themselves to look like fashion models. In each of these cases, people have made their own sense of well-being contingent on others recognizing their success. They're jumping through comparison hoops.

Internet, television, advertising, and other communication media invite us to compare ourselves with others. We are painfully aware that some people have gazillions of dollars and the lifestyles of the rich and famous; we are bombarded with images of supposedly perfect people with perfect faces and bodies; we deify actors and athletes. Invariably, when be begin comparing ourselves to these images, we find ourselves lacking.

When we fall into the comparison trap, we keep the key to real success or well-being out of reach. Clay demonstrates this as he talks with his supervisor, Alice.

"If I don't get the raise I think I deserve, I'm leaving this place."

"Are you talking about your merit increase?" asked Alice.

"Yeah. I'm way below market, so I expect to get to $40,000 this year."

"Wait a second, Clay, isn't your current salary $32,000?"

"Yeah, but I know it's way below market."

"How long have you been in this job, Clay?"

"About a year."

"And if I remember correctly, when you started here, we gave you a 20 percent increase over the position you held at the last company."

"That's right."

"So what makes you think you should suddenly be at $40,000?"

"Because I went into a Website and looked up a job that had a description close to the one for my job. And it says the market rate is $40,000."

"Clay, do you know what the average increase is this year for companies throughout the country?"

"No."

"It's three and a half percent. We're giving an average of five percent. Even if you were the greatest employee I've got, you'd be asking for an increase of 25 percent. I thought you really liked your job."

"I do—in fact I love my job; but I just won't be happy if I don't get $40,000."

"What if you jumped into a job over your head, or one where the people were difficult to work with. Wouldn't you be sorry you left a job you loved for that?"

"No, somehow I'd be happy, because I'd be making $40,000."

Clay has done what so many of us do; he's compared himself to others and decided he falls short. He's placed himself in a position where he really believes that attaining that extra $8,000 will solve all his problems. He'll be happy, somehow, even if the people he works with are horrible or the job is not doable. In reality, should Clay jump to this new position, he'll likely be grumbling within 12 months. The money won't make Clay happy. Only Clay can make Clay happy.

People who constantly compare themselves to others end up leading miserable lives. They are on the worst of all treadmills. Harvey is an attorney in Chicago and is at his worst when he compares himself to others. Listen as he talks with a new attorney, Trina.

"Well, Trina, you've joined one of the best personal injury law firms in the city," Harvey says as he greets her in the reception area. "We're second only to Swartz and Bommarito, and I can't figure out how they get so many deals!" he shouts as he slams his fist down onto a table.

"Well, I'm excited to be here. It took a lot of work to end up 48th in my class."

"That's not bad. How many were in your class?"

"Fifty."

"Oh, I see," Harvey muses with an ever so slight roll of his eyes. "Well, you're in the big leagues now. We have pretty nice offices, don't we?"

"They're beautiful."

"Well it wasn't easy to get into this building—right on the shore of Lake Michigan."

"And on the 37th floor with a spectacular view, "Trina adds.

"Well, it could have been better. Someday we'll be up on the 50th floor, as soon as those morons who rent that space move out. Come into my office and take a look," he says, moving her into a large, well-appointed office.

"This is a beautiful office," Trina sighs, rubbing her hand along the mahogany desk. "Someday maybe I'll have one like it."

Harvey smiles. "Come over here and look at the view," he says as he directs her to the wall of picture windows overlooking a marina on Lake Michigan. "If you look down there, you can see my 50-foot cruiser."

"Where is it?" she asks, searching for a large cruiser among many large cruisers. "Is it that huge one over there? Oh, it's beautiful."

"Uhh, no," he replies sheepishly. "That is a hundred-foot yacht."

"Oh, I guess at this distance, it's hard to tell size," she says apologetically. "I've never been on any kind of cruiser or yacht, so I'm sure a 50-footer is huge—and it probably cost a fortune."

"You don't know the half of it. Look right below us. It's down there," he says, pointing his finger to a white cruiser directly below them.

"It's got a name on it, but I can't quite read it."

"Yeah, I'm really proud of that boat. I worked hard to get it, and I wanted it to represent the spirit of my career. So, I named it after the three words dearest to my heart."

"So, you named it after your wife?"

"Are you kidding?"

"Well, then what is the name? Come on, I can't read it. Please tell me."

"It's the three words dearest to me, and if you're going to be a success in this firm, they'll be the three words dearest to you."

"Please don't keep me guessing. What's the name of your yacht?"

"Slip and fall."

As you might have guessed, Harvey is not a happy person. Despite his wealth and his cruiser, he's jealous and angry about his competitors, and he's embarrassed when his attempt to impress the new recruit backfires as she mistakes his yacht for the hundred-footer. For Harvey, there's always going to be someone who has more than he does, and he's always going to compare himself to them. His life will be a treadmill until he finally decides that his personal success is not a function of his acquisitions.

Do you compare yourself to others to the point that you give them control? Answer the following questions:

- When you achieve a significant goal, do you find yourself unable to enjoy it because you're concerned other people have achieved more ambitious goals?
- When you experience a setback in your life, do you reflexively blame other people for the setback?
- When someone gives you a compliment, do you often respond with false humility, denigrating yourself by saying, "It's nothing compared to what _____ has accomplished."
- When you've resigned from a job, have you done so because you weren't making enough money or enjoying as much prestige as someone else you know?
- When you've gone on a vacation and are having a good time, do you catch yourself thinking something along the lines of, "This is nice, but it's not nearly as _____ (exotic, expensive a trip, glamorous, exciting) as the trip that someone else I know took.

If you find yourself making these comparisons, you're doing something that many of us do. Just becoming aware that you're doing it will help you manage this type of negative behavior. If you can catch and stop yourself from doing it at least some of the time, you'll put yourself in a better position for a personal takeover.

As you have seen throughout this chapter, jumping through hoops takes various forms. It includes hypersensitivity to the messages others give us, applying conditions before we give ourselves permission to feel successful, and defining our personal success through comparisons with others. In all instances, jumping through hoops presents you with a barrier to your own personal takeover. As long as you define success as acquiring more, being accepted or loved by someone, or achieving a certain rank, you've given away the personal power you have to take control over your life.

Chapter 4

The Victim Mindset: How It Limits Your Success

> " *The carousel of life goes round and round,*
> *but I keep falling off.* "

ONE OF THE MOST PROFOUNDLY NEGATIVE MINDSETS IS THE "victim mindset." The self-talk running through victims' heads revolves around how they are not in control (they can't stop bad things from happening to them), that they should not have to accept responsibility for events occurring around them (what's the point?) and that the world around them must be viewed with suspicion (who is going to victimize them next?).

The victim mindset is paralyzing. It robs you of the initiative to take charge of your life. Unconsciously, you're saying to yourself, *Why should I launch a personal takeover? It's just going to end badly. Maybe it sounds like a good idea, but I'm sure I'll mess it up like I've messed everything else up. Or someone else will mess it up.*

Here's an example of the victim mindset in action. Dave, Betty, and Thelma run an accelerated solutions team in Information Technology. They have just pulled their team together for a meeting. Dave starts it off.

"Okay everyone, listen up. You've all had a chance to take a look at this county sewage disposal problem."

"The whole thing stinks if you ask me," said Betty.

"Very funny. Boy, I didn't realize the smell was so bad around the governor's mansion until we took the site visit," said Thelma.

"Well, it wasn't like that before he moved in," replied Dave.

"Listen," Thelma said, "they want something done now. That's why they called us in."

"Well, I've been doing some estimates," said Betty, "and I really don't believe this is that much of a software challenge. I believe I could probably develop a software solution myself that would divert the waste flow. I think it could be done in 60 days. Let's tell them we'll have it by June 1st."

"Bite your tongue!" snapped Dave. "Don't you know that an IT team never gives a date to the client? Remember, clients don't appreciate technology people. You start throwing out dates, and when things bog down in the software development, they're going to try to hold us accountable to actually meet them!"

"Come on, Dave," said Thelma. "We have to tell them something. I suggest we tell them it will take three years. By then, the governor will be out of office."

"Good idea, Thelma. Maybe then the problem will just go away. I can't believe we got stuck with this high profile problem. Someone's trying to get rid of us."

Dave and Thelma are both exhibiting forms of the victim mindset. Whereas Betty is optimistic about the timing on the software development, both Dave and Thelma want to avoid accountability and are convinced someone else will nail them if they commit to a deadline. Dave holds onto a mindset that "clients don't appreciate technology people."

The victim mindset can take many different forms, and those of us who have victim mindsets will display various behaviors, providing others with clues to the fact that we're viewing the world from the victim's perspective. Let's look at the most common types and what you can do if you catch yourself thinking in victim terms.

The cynic mindset

Cynics view the world through the lens of Murphy's Law: If something can go wrong, it will go wrong. They put people down and make fun of those who are positive and idealistic. Humor is often a great response to difficult situations, but cynics use it to discourage and discredit. Like Dave, cynics use humor as a way of avoiding accountability, turning everything into a snide remark. They don't trust what the world has to offer, and their thoughts focus on mere survival. Hard-core cynics verge on the paranoid, convinced that the world is against them. They fully expect to come up short because it's them versus the world, and this expectation is often fulfilled.

Scenario

Georgia prides herself on her cynical view. She's a 12th grade English teacher who has been teaching at the same school for over a decade. Recently, she attended a staff meeting called by the Principal of her school. The Principal began by explaining that the meeting's purpose was to introduce new testing procedures mandated by the district and designed to ensure more students would pass the state proficiency exams.

"As if he really cares," whispered Georgia to a teacher next to her. "If he could spell himself, he would have spelled the word *resignation* a long time ago."

"I know this is going to be hard for all of us, with the extra work and all," the Principal continued.

"Oh, are you going to join me in my classroom?" mumbled Georgia, unfortunately loud enough for the Principal to hear.

"In fact, I plan to have all of the administrative staff, including myself, join you in your classrooms as often as possible to assist you in any way we can."

"So you can get in our way, bungle everything up, and then make sure we take the blame," Georgia whispered.

Cynics like Georgia are rarely challenged. Most people give them pass, and they're free to undermine others who are enthusiastic or who are trying to make things better. Cynics are tolerated partly because no one wants to draw attention to themselves and come under the cynics' attack. Sometimes, too, cynics are appreciated for their intelligence and humor. People like Georgia can be clever when they make their cynical asides, and their bosses may rationalize their negative remarks as a necessary dose of realism.

The reality is that cynics are terribly afraid of being victimized, and this fear keeps them from having the courage to launch a takeover. Their caustic comments are driven by fearful thoughts about what's going to happen next or who's going to try and take advantage of them. They are constantly engaging in self-talk like, *What's behind that comment?* and thinking it in a sneering tone. When they meet someone new, they don't think that it's a great opportunity to meet someone with fresh ideas and different experiences. Instead, they start questioning the motives behind anything they say or do, even the most innocent of statements.

If you catch yourself thinking in this cynical mode or translating your thoughts into cynical words or deeds, here are two ways to moderate this unproductive, counter-takeover mindset:

- **Confront your fears.** Fears turn to cynicism when they're unexamined. Make an effort to articulate what scares you, either in writing (in a journal) or in conversations with others. Simply stating that you're terrified of being downsized or that you're afraid of a competitor's new, aggressive approach will make it less likely that you'll resort to cynicism. Once the fear is out in the open, it has less power, and you won't feel as great a need to avoid its terrible power through a cynical thought or remark.

- **Make a list of the most successful people you know and determine which ones are cynics**. The odds are that very few cynics, if any, will show up on your list. If you examine the ranks of corporate CEOs, entrepreneurs who have built businesses, well-respected doctors, politicians, and consultants, for the most part, you'll find people who are idealistic, work well with others, and are willing to extend trust in relationships. Rarely will you find cynics.

The win-lose mindset

People who hold the win-lose mindset see the world as a place of scarcity. If you get more, then I get less. When they view the world in this way, they're convinced that every time they have an opportunity to acquire something, it's going to be at somebody else's expense. If somebody else has something to gain, it's at their expense. This type of victim mindset creates adversarial relationships with everyone—coworkers, direct reports (subordinates), bosses, and suppliers. Resources are scarce, so cutthroat competition is necessary for them to get their fair share.

Sean is the head of a lending group for a large commercial bank, and his group has put together a campaign to attract new business loans. For this reason, Sean made an appointment with Faith, the head of the Credit Department, to discuss how they might expedite processing the loan requests his group solicits.

"Faith, I was hoping your group could help us with our new loan campaign," Sean said. "We've set a goal to place 100 new loans in the next three months at a total outstanding balance of $50 million."

"How are we going to help?" Faith asked, but thought, *I don't like this guy—I never have. He's always coming up with some kind of new campaign. Always out there, leading the charge, the jerk.*

"Well, normally it takes a week to get the analysis, approval, and all the paperwork done on a new loan request. I was wondering if your group could work with us to process these in an average of two days each. The bank is really struggling right now, and if we could do this together, it might create momentum for the rest of the bank." As he said this, Sean thought, *Hopefully that will sell her. The idea of it helping the whole bank sounds good, though she's always leery of everything.*

"There's no way we're going to process your loans in two days," said Faith. "We've decided to focus on quality, so frankly, processing time is likely to double to two weeks." She thought, *There, I've stopped you cold. I love to throw roadblocks in front of you. You're too high and mighty.*

"You're kidding. Our customers aren't going to put up with that. They'll leave us." Sean thought, *I've got to come up with what's in it for her.*

This win-lose approach becomes a self-fulfilling prophecy. When people work together and one of them sees the other continually competing for resources with a winner-take-all approach, the other person is going to respond with the same win-lose mentality. It becomes a vicious cycle, with each person convinced that it's all or nothing.

If you think you hold some of the win-lose mindset, try the following:

- **Read about the Middle East conflict, the Kashmir conflict between India and Pakistan, or Richard Nixon.** President Nixon, like the countries in the two conflicts, divided the world into winners and losers. They all believed the old western adage that, "This town ain't big enough for the both of us." When you realize the consequences of this type of thinking, you see how it ultimately turns everyone into a loser.

- **Create an enemies list.** On a piece of paper, note all the people who you're feuding with in work-related situations (bosses, employees, coworkers, customers/clients, suppliers). Go through each person on the list and answer the following questions: Is this individual a horrible, hateful person who would gladly see me hurt? Did this person become my enemy because he or she did something horrible to me? Might this individual be an okay person, who I have transformed into an enemy? While you may have a legitimate foe or two, a little analysis often reveals that the win-lose mindset often blows minor incidents out of proportion.

The pawn mindset

Pawns feel they have no control over their lives, as evidenced by their external locus of control. When we have an external locus of control, we see control as outside of us and believe we are at the mercy of other people, events, and change. Just as in a game of chess, pawns see themselves with very few options, with limited chance of movement, and with the likelihood that they'll be the first to be taken. Pawns often believe fate is why things happen to them. If something goes wrong, they are fatalistic about it, convinced it wasn't their own doing.

We can see this played out in an organizational setting when employees with pawn mindsets are dissatisfied. In most instances, they complain to others rather than bringing the issue to their managers for discussion. When asked, "Why didn't you bring this issue up with us or try to change it?" the typical response is, "Why try? It wouldn't make any difference anyway." As victims, pawns are resigned to being out of the loop and unable to impact decisions.

There was a show on television in the 1950s called "Queen for a Day." The format of the show was for several women to talk about all of the setbacks they had experienced. The woman demonstrating that she had the most setbacks was crowned queen for a day and would receive prizes and pampering.

Today, we find many people who take an almost perverse pleasure in all the bad things that happen to them. Instead of receiving prizes and pampering, however, they get to say, "See, I knew this was going to happen." Psychologically, this is not healthy. In fact, psychologists say depression results from feelings of lack of control. Pawns often question their ability to be in control of some aspect of their life and may even believe the world is set against them. The stronger this feeling is, the more likely it is that they're depressed.

Experience shows that we get over 90 percent of the things we request. The remaining low probability of being rejected, however, results in pawns being unwilling to make an effort. The pawn mindset means that thoughts of being rejected keep building up to the point that people cling to the status quo. In organizations, pawns are change-resisters; they will expend tremendous amounts of energy to avoid doing something new or different.

If you have a pawn mentality, you can combat it by:

- **Playing your own version of chess**. Obtain a pawn and a king or queen from a chess set, keep them on your desk, and ask yourself, *Which one would I rather be?* You might also keep a list of traits of pawns, which includes: limited movement, easily sacrificed, and interchangeable.

- **Practice thinking like a "mover" rather than a "movee."** Be alert for thoughts of helplessness and self-pity. When you hear yourself thinking, *Woe is me*, force yourself to write down what you might do to alter a given situation. Even if what you might do is a small thing, note the possibility. If you do this consistently, you'll realize that you're not a pawn and that you do have power to "change the board."

The glass half-empty mindset

People with the glass half-empty mindset focus on the downside of any event or circumstance.

Scenario

Terry is a glass half-empty person. He supervises a group of programmers for the city and was recently asked to communicate a new initiative for all city employees to dress in business attire when they meet with the public or companies that are considering relocating to the city. After many years of effort, the city was finally attracting businesses to relocate there, and the mayor wanted to make sure that the city workers presented a professional image. When informed of this initiative, he told his boss, Michelle, that programmers wouldn't like having to wear business attire.

"What if we point out that we're trying to show the rest of the world that this city has very professional people?" asked Michelle.

"My group will say, if you want us to act more professional, pay us more."

"Come on, Terry. That's ridiculous. The city pays pretty well. Plus, we're going to have additional funds for pay hikes if we keep getting more companies to relocate here."

"I can't believe more companies are going to move to this city. Companies don't want to relocate here because of the depressed economy."

"That's precisely why they want to be here. Companies feel they can attract people at a slightly lower rate of pay than in other parts of the state. So, don't you think you can give your team a real sell on why they should dress professionally?"

"If I do, they'll think I'm a hypocrite. They know I don't even own a suit. Plus, they're going to be upset about all the new business the city is getting. It means they're going to have to work a lot harder, which some of them won't be thrilled about. I see trouble ahead."

Terry is one of those people who can find the negative side of even the best information. I have seen employees turn down grants of company stock that would have had no cost to them because they were convinced there was some negative angle that had not been communicated. In one company, an employee refused to accept a grant of 20,000 shares of stock that today would be worth approximately $400,000.

Here's a good response to these anti-takeover thoughts:

- **Turn a half-empty thought into a half-full one.** This doesn't mean putting a positive spin on a terrible tragedy. Instead, focus on an event or situation that is only moderately upsetting. Perhaps your boss made a negative remark in an otherwise positive performance review or you lost a customer you were certain you were going to get. Concentrate on thinking about what positives you can take away from the experience.

For instance: *Next time I'll provide a prospect with more information to avoid having them turn me down because I wasn't "thorough enough."*

The chronic complainer mindset

People who are always griping about their jobs, their salaries, their competitors, and their customers set up a verbal barrier to a takeover. They literally talk themselves into believing that there are too many things wrong in their life for them to gain power over their jobs and careers. The chronic complainer is unhappy about general circumstances and is actually unwilling to take charge. They don't want to take the risk of standing out in front and being a leader. As a chronic complainer, they can sit back and take potshots at others.

Scenario

Lori, having dinner with her best friend, Sharon, was in the process of telling Sharon that her life was terrible.

"What's wrong?" asked Sharon.

"Well, first of all, my work is so boring. I can't stand it. I sit around all day. I have about three hours worth of work to spread over eight hours."

"Lori, you've been complaining about your job for years. Why don't you talk with your manager about this? Maybe she can help you somehow."

"Are you kidding? All the managers at my company are idiots. And my boss is the worst. She's great at playing politics, but she's a lousy manager."

"Oh come on, Lori, it can't be that bad," Sharon said, trying to coax Lori into looking at the bright side.

"Well it is, and our quality is going right down the tube. We're losing customers left and right."

"But, Lori, I thought you were in charge of quality."

"They don't give me any authority. They make all the decisions."

"Don't you think it's time you started looking for something you could enjoy?"

"You don't understand, Sharon. There aren't a lot of jobs out there that pay the kind of money I make for the little work I do."

"Yeah, but you hate it! Listen, you always said you'd like to be a teacher. Why don't you do that?"

"I'd have to go back to school. It would take too long. Plus, I wouldn't be able to make the money I'm making now. It would take me a good five years to just get back to my current salary. Listen, I don't want to talk about work anymore. It's too depressing. Let's talk about something else."

"Okay," replied Sharon, "how's your love life?"

"It's terrible."

As you can see in the dialogue above, Lori has an answer for every suggestion Sharon gives. Unfortunately, the answer is always a negative one. The chronic complainer displays the victim mindset in spades. Lori's view of things prevents any real positive movement in her life.

If you catch yourself complaining chronically—either to others or to yourself—try the following:

- **Give yourself the "punishment" of one thankful thought for every complaining one.** When you catch yourself complaining about work or other people, find something to be thankful for (related to what you were complaining about). If you were complaining about something your boss did, think of something that he or she did that made your grateful or happy in some way.
- **Identify your biggest complaint.** What are you always grousing about? Who are you always telling yourself has "done you wrong"? What complaining theme keeps resurfacing in your mind? Whatever this person

or theme is, determine what good all this complaining has done you. Specify the benefit of spending hours, days, or weeks in total complaining about this single subject. If you're like most people, you'll realize that all this complaining was a gigantic waste of time.

The blame-shifter mindset

Responsibility is critical to a successful takeover. Blame-shifters avoid responsibility. If something goes wrong, they start thinking about how to excuse themselves and use others as scapegoats. They expend their energy on finding someone to blame rather than solving the problem that caused things to go wrong.

While working with one of our client companies, an employee referred to a manager as "Teflon Don." When I asked what he was referring to, the employee responded, "Oh, nothing ever sticks to him. He's great at finding scapegoats whenever a problem occurs." When someone avoids responsibility, they're thinking, *You're going to blame me, so I want to blame you first.* They don't realize that this type of thinking prevents them from being heroes and solving problems.

If you want to avoid blame-shifting thinking, here's a simple thing you can do:

- **The next time something goes wrong at work, blame yourself in a positive way.** Maybe a deadline is missed or a report receives a poor reception. Whatever the problem, you'll probably find yourself reflexively pointing your finger. Instead, say something to yourself along the following lines: *Certainly other people were involved in this screw-up, but I have the experience and expertise that I might have prevented it from happening. With hindsight, I know I might have been able to head off the problem or at least minimize the damage. So I accept the blame, but in doing so I also accept my power to solve problems.*

The work-avoider mindset

Being committed to work is crucial for a personal take-over. It means that people have accepted responsibility for what they do and are excited and energized about achieving their goals. They are going to give their all, pulling out all the stops to accomplish a task. Work avoiders, on the other hand, see their jobs as a necessary evil and are rarely committed. They lack the sense of responsibility, energy, and commitment that a personal takeover demands. They spend a lot of time thinking about how to avoid taking control of their work rather than how they might regain control.

Dan does just enough to get by. In his early years with a large packaged goods company, he worked hard and effectively, eventually resulting in his current managerial position. Over time, however, Dan started slacking off. He discovered that there weren't any immediate repercussions to doing less. Astutely, Dan assessed what was critical in his job and what was not, and everything in the latter category was done in a slapdash fashion or shifted onto the shoulders of his direct reports.

It almost became a game for Dan. He would invent ingenious excuses to be out of the office, such as going to trade shows that were really unnecessary or visiting other offices instead of simply making phone calls to obtain the information he needed. Dan, however, found that being out of the office gave him greater latitude to avoid work. He might spend an hour at a trade show and the rest of the day watching television in his hotel room. When he was in the office, Dan spent an inordinate amount of time making personal phone calls and exchanging e-mails with friends. He even bragged to family members that he had mastered the art of "looking like I'm working when I'm not."

Dan didn't seem to care that he wasn't advancing in his career or receiving much satisfaction from his job. Even though he wasn't particularly happy, he assumed he would be even less happy if he worked harder.

If this is your mindset, but you've found it's really not very satisfying, and you'd really like to begin a personal takeover, you might want to do the following:

- **Change some aspect of your work situation**. This doesn't necessarily mean changing jobs (though that might be an option). But it may require you to talk to your boss about providing you with a new project that you can get excited about. It may necessitate a transfer to another team or group in the company. It may involve taking a training course or a class at a local university to develop new skills and knowledge. Whatever it is, you want to shift your mindset away from thoughts about avoiding work and toward thoughts where you're excited about and committed to your work.

The bored mindset

There was a story recently in the news about a couple who were injured when dynamite exploded in the backseat of their car. They were driving out in the country and were bored. So, they decided to light a quarter stick of dynamite and throw it out the window. Except the window was closed. The dynamite hit the window, bounced back into the rear seat, and exploded.

The bored mindset is displayed by individuals like these, who approach work like a country drive. They tend to be activity-driven instead of results-oriented; their thoughts aren't focused and they shy away from reflection, analysis, and planning—all crucial thought processes for a personal takeover. At work, they think about tasks rather than outcomes. Bored individuals sometimes like to stir things up (like the couple with the dynamite) and create a little excitement. Bored with their jobs and careers, they are likely to think a

lot about retirement or what they're going to do on weekends
or at the end of the work day.

If you're bored and have difficulty focusing on and analyzing work issues, try the following:

- **Connect your outside interests to your career or job**.
  What are you interested in? What can't you wait to
  do? Some people live for their fishing trips while others get tremendous satisfaction out of their Yoga
  classes. For many people, it's financially difficult to
  turn hobbies into vocations, so it may be impractical
  (at least at the moment) for you to become a fishing
  guide or Yoga instructor. But it is quite possible to
  search for a job or a specific work task that relates to
  these outside interests. Instead of selling computers,
  maybe you should be selling fishing gear. At the very
  least, explore the possibilities of doing something for
  a living where you're intellectually and emotionally
  engaged in the activity.

- **Analyze why you're bored**. Sometimes the bored
  mindset can be managed when the reasons for being
  bored are uncovered. If you're like most people, you
  don't think about why you're bored—you just complain about it or accept it as a fact of life. In fact, people
  are bored for very specific reasons: they're no longer
  challenged by their work; they aren't learning anything
  new; they see no real payoff for the work they're doing. Recognizing why you're bored gives you a way
  to attack the boredom and to reengage with your job
  and your career.

The critic mindset

Critics rarely look at themselves as the cause of any problem. They reflexively look outward for the cause and are quick
to point out what others are doing wrong or how they've failed.

Many times, they ascribe problems to the bad intentions of others or circumstances beyond their control. They believe self-criticism is unnecessary because they don't hold themselves responsible when things go wrong.

Because of this mindset, critics cannot complete personal takeovers because they assume "others" or outside events are responsible for what happens to them. They often feel the need to find others bungling the work, so that blame can never come back to them. Until they stop looking outside of themselves for causes, they'll be barred from takeovers.

Scenario

Jonathan, a computer programmer, is a critic. Pam, another employee in his organization, approached him about a new program he is writing for her group and asked him how close he was to finishing.

"It's not even started."

"What do you mean it's not even started? Jonathan, you have been working on this for two months!"

"Your group has not performed the business analysis and hasn't completed the specifications document," Jonathan said.

"I didn't know we had to do that."

"Well, that's a problem now, isn't it? Your group doesn't do things like the rest of the organization. That's why you have so many problems."

"Wait a minute, Jonathan! That's unfair. It would be one thing if I knew I needed to do a business analysis and didn't do it. But, don't you think you should have told me I needed to get you a specifications document?"

"That's not my job. Besides, you should know this. You've been at the organization for a number of years, and if you didn't know, someone in your department should have told you. That's part of the problem—no communication in your department."

Rather than deal with the real issue—how he can help solve
the problem—Jonathan is thinking and talking about why others are at fault. Critics like Jonathan rarely look at themselves.
They protect themselves through an assault on others, sometimes to such a degree that people shy away from contact because they want to avoid coming into their line of fire.

To avoid this overly critical thought process, here's a relatively easy way to moderate this mindset:

- **Put the shoe on the other foot**. As a role-playing exercise, ask someone you trust—a spouse, a friend, someone you're close with at work—to take a minute or two
  and be highly critical of you. They don't have to be fair
  or even honest in their criticism. The idea is for them to
  let you have it with both barrels and for you to experience what it feels like. This might make you think twice
  before engaging in overly critical behavior.

The list: find your types

Below you'll find a complete listing of characteristics of
the victim mindset. As you can see, these characteristics over-
lap. For instance, chronic complainers are often highly critical, and people who are bored are often work avoiders. You
may find yourself engaging in more than one of these behaviors or attitudes at different times.

As you review this victim mindset list, focus not only on
yourself but on others you know and work with. Think of a
person who displays many of these unproductive characteristics described, and reflect on the following questions:

- What is the impact on the organization when people
  think like this?
- What is the impact on you when you are around this
  person?
- How does this person affect the energy of the people
  he works with?

- Can you see how difficult it might be for this individual to assume control of his or her life via a personal takeover?

Characteristics of Victim Mindsets

The cynic
- Takes a cynical view toward the world.
- Focuses on survival and sees self against the world.
- Questions motives and is suspicious of others.

The win-lose individual
- Sees a world of scarcity.
- Competes with coworkers for people and resources.
- Addresses problems or issues in an adversarial way.

The pawn
- Possesses an external locus of control, seeing control outside of self, thus resulting in statements like, "You're the reason I'm this way."
- Displays a "poor me" attitude.
- Attributes events to fate, and responds with statements like, "Why try? It wouldn't be approved anyway."

The glass half-empty individual
- Chooses to see the negative side of any situation.
- Finds it difficult to get beyond the problem, so rarely finds a solution.
- Focuses on what *won't* work instead of what *will* work.

The blame-shifter
- Avoids responsibility.
- Shifts the blame to others when problems arise.
- Seeks scapegoats when things go wrong.

The chronic complainer
- Displays an unwillingness to take charge or lead efforts.
- Complains continually without providing solutions.
- Sows negativity in the organization and helps breed discontent.

cont'd

Characteristics of Victim Mindsets, *cont'd*

The work-avoider
- Sees work as necessary evil.
- Spends large amounts of time on personal or social activities instead of the work itself.
- Fails to volunteer to do anything beyond the assigned tasks.

The bored individual
- Shows little initiative in keeping self interested.
- Expects to be entertained.
- Utilizes all personal, vacation, and sick time available and tries to find more.

The critic
- Criticizes other people and discounts their efforts.
- Sees self as being better than everyone else.
- Makes openly critical comments about the organization.

All of us engage in some victim thinking

People rarely have all of these negative characteristics, but every one of us has some of them some of the time. There is no person, no matter how positive or successful, who is not going to have some of these feelings at times. That is part of being human. It is totally natural.

As I described the different characteristics of victim mindsets in the previous examples, you should have been able to identify some situations that were familiar. You might have also discovered that your own victim thinking is contextual. For instance, you might be a critic in the business world, but be very positive and supportive with members of your family. It's also possible that you're bored when engaged in certain work assignments and not bored when doing other tasks, yet you've made no effort to make your overall work more exciting.

The point of this chapter, and the previous ones, has been to raise your awareness of how your beliefs and view of the world are correlated with your sense of well-being and your personal success. Your mindsets have impacted how you act, and those actions have yielded certain results. If you've looked at the world through the lens of the victim, things have probably looked pretty bleak. Depending on the degree to which you've led your life conditionally, or based on comparison with others, you've probably felt like you've jumped through an awful lot of hoops. This leads us to takeover rule #7.

☑ Takeover Rule #7: ☑

If you look at the world through the lens of the victim, things will probably look pretty bleak. If you are living your life conditionally, you are jumping through a lot of hoops. Yelp, yelp!

The good news, however, is that your awareness of the impact of these unproductive approaches has been raised. Now it's a matter of deciding to do something about them. Transitioning from a victim to a takeover mindset is a process, and this process begins with "making yourself an offer."

Chapter 5

Making Yourself an Offer:
How to Start the Takeover

" " *I've been ringing the bell, but you ain't*
fixin' my life, so I'm fixin' to leave."

H AVING WARMED UP YOUR TAKEOVER MUSCLES, YOU'RE NOW
ready to make yourself an offer. Though this is just the start of
the process, it's an important step. You're offering yourself
the opportunity to stop thinking like a victim and start thinking more productively. You've already glimpsed what the takeover mindset is like. It's the ability to place yourself in charge
of what happens to you and believe that you have the capacity
to shape the course of your life in any way you choose.

Admittedly, the ramifications of this offer may feel scary.
It takes courage to challenge a mindset you've held probably
most of your life. When you take over your life, you take the
risk of assuming responsibility for your actions. For this reason, I'm not going to ask you to make this offer until the end
of the chapter. There are a few things that will be helpful to
learn first and some exercises that will be useful to perform.

Let's begin by learning why thinking like a victim is often
something we're conditioned to do.

Victims from birth

One of the early experimenters in conditioned response was Ivan Pavlov. Pavlov became famous for his experiments with dogs. Pavlov would ring a bell and feed a dog at the same time. After doing this repeatedly, Pavlov conditioned the dog to expect food any time the bell would ring. Pavlov next subtracted food from the equation. He merely rang the bell and studied the dog's response. The dog, expecting to be fed, began salivating.

Babies learn the idea of conditioned response quite quickly. It comes in the form of tears. Babies are hungry or uncomfortable. What do they do? They cry. What is the response? Adults come rushing into their rooms to take care of them—to hold them, feed them, change their diapers. The babies learn that when they want something, all they have to do is cry.

By the time children are five years old, they have been rewarded thousands of times for crying. They have also learned that, should they want something done, they merely need to cry and someone will take care of it for them. It's somebody else's responsibility to fix things, not theirs.

Although most of us hear the words *personal responsibility* while growing up, we have been rewarded so many times for whining and playing the victim, we have difficulty changing our approach. In the world of business, perhaps more than any other, many of us believe that our boss or some other "higher-up" is responsible for fixing things, even if we are part of the cause for something going wrong.

To glimpse how ingrained this response is, think of a recent snafu at work. Maybe a customer called to complain because of a service problem, or perhaps your team had conflicts you couldn't manage and a meeting degenerated into a hostile argument. With this in mind, answer the following questions:

- When the problem flared up, did you ignore it, hoping it would just go away?
- Did you try to distance yourself from the problem, hoping someone else would fix it?
- Did you contact your boss and expect him to fix it?
- Did you feel that the problem or failure was so complex that you were incapable of dealing with it on your own?
- Did you feel the situation was too important for you to be able to handle it on your own?
- Thinking about who was best able to remedy the situation, did you attribute almost magical powers to your boss or someone else higher up in the organization? Do you think of a certain executive as a Mr. or Ms. Fix-it, capable of handling almost anything?

If you answered yes to some or all of these questions, accept that your response might just have its origins all the way back to those first days in the crib. Avoiding taking action, or looking to someone else to fix the problem, is akin to the baby deciding it's time to cry because we have a situation here that needs attention. To make yourself an offer and begin a personal takeover, you need to get past this type of conditioned response. The following story may help you see why it's so important to be conscious of this response and make an effort to overcome it.

Public execution:
resist the "ready, aim, fire" impulse

Scenario

I was running a three-day retreat for a group of employees within my own organization. During one of the discussion periods, an employee brought up an issue with another employee back at the company. The dialogue went something like this:

"Darnita is not a very pleasant person to work with. I mean, she doesn't even say good morning to you when you pass her in the hallway," Phyllis said.

"Yeah, I noticed that. She is quite rude," added Janelle.

"She's a pretty good worker, though," said Byron. "She's always been real responsive when I've asked her for anything. I will agree, though, that she can be pretty confrontational. One time when we were working on a project together, she and I really got into it over how we were going to structure the project plan. I almost quit because of the way she talked to me."

"That's terrible," responded Phyllis. "Something should be done about Darnita."

At this point, I felt the dialogue had led us to a point where we might all be able to learn something about unproductive approaches.

"What should be done?" I asked.

"I don't know—but somebody should do something about that person," insisted Janelle.

"Have any of you talked with Darnita about her approach?" I asked.

"That's not our job! It's her manager's job to address that!" Phyllis said.

"But if you're the one who has experienced her rudeness, why wouldn't you be the person to address it with her?" I asked.

"I'm not paid to do that. You guys are paid to do that," Byron explained.

"So I should confront Darnita, or your manager should confront her, when it's you who feels she is being rude?" I asked.

"Yes, that's right," said Janelle.

"Well, let me ask you this: What consequence should Darnita receive as a result of her being rude to you?"

"I don't know, but a person who acts like that doesn't belong here," said Phyllis.

"So, maybe I should fire her?"

"If she can't change the way she talks to people...."

The conversation continued in this vein for another half hour. There were actually about eight employees in the room with me. I told them I wanted to use this conversation as a learning tool. I began by telling them that their frustration with Darnita was understandable. I also pointed out that when one employee has an issue with another employee, it's always uncomfortable to address. It is not unusual for us to desire that somebody else address the issue instead of us doing it.

But, then I took this discussion to another level. I told them that throughout my years as a manager, I regularly have had people in my office who had an issue with somebody else in the organization. Sometimes the other employee had not performed his part of the job; other times it was a conflict or disagreement that prompted the meeting; and, in some cases, an individual was upset because she was fed up with the way her coworker acted (what some people refer to as a "personality conflict"). No matter what the cause of their visit to my office might have been, they usually responded in a similar manner when asked what they'd like me to "do" to the other person: They desired a reprimand at the very least. In reality, what they probably wanted was for me to fire the offending party or subject her to some form of public humiliation.

Public humiliation sounds extreme, doesn't it? But it's exactly how many victim-minded people feel when they clash with their fellow workers. Haven't you ever heard employees grumble about someone else, and then follow their grumbling with a statement like, "I don't think management is even doing anything about her." While most of us want our own bosses to address an issue they have with us privately, when it comes to others, we want to know something is being done. We want it public.

I call this the *public execution*. People who succumb to victim thinking want to see a public execution of an offending employee, particularly if that offending employee has rubbed them the wrong way. The unfortunate manager who does provide his people with what they want—who actually does publicize what is being done to reprimand an employee—finds that the tables quickly turn on him. Employees clamoring to see a public execution are suddenly aghast, saying things like "If he tells us how he is reprimanding her, then he's unlikely to keep what I say to him confidential."

During our employee retreat, I attempted to make these points, explaining that they all wanted to see Darnita executed in public. I asked them each if they didn't, in fact, harbor some desire to see Darnita terminated. They all acknowledged that, at least to some degree, they did.

Then I said, "Do you know that at one time or another, someone has wanted to see each and every one of us fired?"

The entire group was shocked at my statement. How could others have wanted them fired? I proceeded to go around the room, taking each person at a time, and recited the incident that caused someone else to want them terminated.

All of these people were good performers. A few of them were star performers. But some of them had struggled earlier in their careers. One, a single parent, had experienced day care problems when she first joined the organization. She was almost terminated due to her struggle to keep to the work schedule. Today, she is a manager of a large area and has been very successful, but even she has not always been tolerant of new employees who had difficulty maintaining work schedules.

Another individual had struggled in her first assignment with the organization after graduating from college. Her coworkers became impatient with her and began suggesting she be terminated. Luckily for her, the supervisor of that area believed in her potential and negotiated a move to another position. Today she manages a number of people in the organization.

I know there have been times when some people in our organization would have nominated me for public execution; they probably were convinced that I was leading the company into the abyss and the only remedy was to push me out before I dragged the company in that direction.

Think about the implications of this desire for a public execution. If we all were to act on this desire for a figurative beheading every time conflicts or problems with other people surface, none of us would be here. We are all human beings and are imperfect by our very nature. We usually accept this in ourselves, but we have difficulty accepting it in others. We're convinced others should match the reality we have created, and if they don't, we feel they are "wrong for the job" or the organization.

This is the victim mindset, pure and simple, when we employ conditioned response to conflict and adversity. Rather than believing we can control and resolve the situation ourselves, we take the easy way out and hope our bosses can eliminate the problem. At one time or another, all of us have wished that someone we work with would be executed publicly. A victim mindset, however, causes us to act on this wish consistently. We tell others that someone should be terminated or take actions to increase the odds of it happening. A takeover mindset, however, would cause us to act differently. It would hold us accountable to resolve the situation on our own.

☑ Takeover Rule #8: ☑

Don't look to others to take care of your problems.

Think about how you feel about the people with whom you work most closely. Do you want some or even all of them executed in public? If so, it's going to be tough for you to make yourself a takeover offer. If, on the other hand, you recognize the possibility of dealing with personal conflicts and problems yourself, then you have a much greater chance of pulling off this offer.

Therefore, learn to manage the execution impulse by doing the following:

1. Name someone you work with who you're convinced should be verbally reprimanded in front of your group or censured in some other public manner.

2. Explain why this person deserves this public execution—provide a succinct reason that justifies this action.

3. Think about whether vengeance or hostility toward this individual is what motivates your desire for this action to take place.

4. Consider whether this public execution would help you achieve your career goals.

5. Identify an alternative in which you, rather than someone else, handle whatever issues exist between you and this other individual.

After taking the five actions suggested above, you'll probably see that having someone publicly executed benefits no one and rarely solves your problems.

Refusing to be guided by the media or your past

Emerging from a victim mindset to the point that you can make yourself an offer requires overcoming the influence of the media and your past. In terms of the former, we are barraged by information on a daily basis that convinces us we're victims; the media encourage us to embrace the victim mindsets described in the last chapter. I randomly chose the *Los Angeles Times* for several days in April 2002, and some of the articles I encountered documented the following: an attempted coup in Afghanistan (win-lose); President Bush unhappy with lack of leadership by Israel or the Palestinian Authority (critic); occupation of the left bank by Israel (win-lose); inability of Yassir Arafat to leave his compound (pawn); belief that the players can't work things out without the United States (pawn); mutual hatred of Palestinians and Jews as evidenced by bombings and buildings being defaced in France (win-lose); Enron executive and his wealth (cynic, comparison). This is just a small sampling and is not meant to single out the *Los Angeles Times*. It is no different from any other national daily in its coverage, and it tries to be responsible. Still, they know what sells. People don't want to have a constant diet of feel-good stories about boy scouts who help little old ladies across the street. They'd much rather hear about scandals, atrocities, and other sensational events.

Being exposed to all this bad news day after day warps our sense of reality. We expect bad things to happen. We become convinced that we're going to be carjacked, that we're going to get a terrible disease, and that we're going to be swindled out of our life savings. The media contribute to the feeling that these awful things happen to everyone all the time, failing to balance these tragedies with positive news.

The other thing we need to overcome is our past. Let's face it. Life is a journey along a very bumpy road. We each battle with illness, disease, crime, accidents, and personal failures. When a failure occurs, it's understandable for us to wonder what's wrong with us. It's normal to fall into a slump. It's quite easy and natural to feel that some greater powers are working against us. This is often reflected in the lament, "Why me?"

When somebody does something that results in us getting hurt, it can be very difficult to drop the negative feelings about the incident or the person. The roles we play in life automatically place us in situations where the dynamics of our interactions can lead to a victim feeling. We see this in the relationships between employer and employee, husband and wife, parent and child, seller and purchaser, and others.

It is very difficult to drop the feelings of anger and hurt after you have felt victimized. Many of us hold onto these feelings for many years after the event actually occurred. In some cases, we carry these feelings to our death. The sad part about this is that holding onto these feelings causes us to be living our lives today based on something that happened to us in the past. We are, in essence, living in the past. We're living based on memories, instead of the present day.

☑ Takeover Rule #9: ☑

***Don't live your life today
based upon memories from the past.***

The following is a list of memories that keep us bogged down in the past. See which ones apply to you:

- A contentious divorce or other type of hostile relationship breakup.
- Being fired from a job.
- Receiving a bad performance review or other negative comments from a boss.
- Being sued.
- Having someone try to take advantage of you in a business transaction.
- A parent saying or doing something you consider cruel or unfair.
- A child saying or doing something you consider cruel or unfair.

Whatever memories apply to you, think about how long ago the incident (or incidents) took place and whether the intensity of the feeling it engendered is such that it feels like it happened yesterday. Ask yourself why you're holding on to such a negative feeling and what purpose it serves. Make a conscious effort to let go of this feeling of victimization.

Learning to escape the drama triangle rather than letting it confine you

To get to the point that you can make a takeover offer to yourself, you need to be aware of and rise above the drama triangle that is all too common in the workplace. Even if you learn to cope with your past experiences and media messages that have encouraged a victim mentality, the drama triangle can still keep you stuck. Let's look at what this triangle is and what you can do to escape its grasp.

Stephen Karpman developed the drama triangle to represent unhealthy roles played within families. As shown in the figure that follows, the three roles played are persecutor, rescuer, and victim.

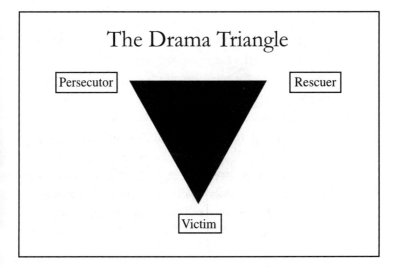

This concept of the drama triangle has been used extensively in family therapy. Victims see themselves as powerless and the unfortunate recipient of some unfair action, event, or decision. Interestingly, they also have the majority of power in this triangle because others are revolving around them. In family therapy, the rescuer is the member of the family who wants to take care of things for the victim and who tries to defend the victim from the persecutor. Rescuers do this out of a need to feel wanted, and often see themselves as above the others. The persecutor is typically the family member who is angry with the victim, and often verbally or physically abuses the victim.

This same type of triangular drama surfaces when people act out dysfunctional roles within the work place. It typically starts out with someone who takes on the role of the victim. When someone does this, it opens the opportunity for others to jump in and act out the corresponding roles of persecutor and rescuer. And each of the players can switch roles. The victim can become the persecutor, the persecutor can become the rescuer, and the rescuer can become the victim. The switching of roles keeps the drama alive.

The following are traits of each of these three roles:

Persecutors
- Make personally attacking statements about victims.
- Criticize victims for not doing something.
- Show up late for meetings with someone they view as a victim.
- Disregard statements made by victims.
- Don't respond to phone calls or e-mails from victims.
- Initiate conflicts or disagreements with victims.
- Demand that victims be disciplined or punished by the organization, preferably resulting in public humiliation.

Rescuers

- Attempt to smooth over conflicts between victims and persecutors.
- Listen and console victims without challenging them.
- Do extra work that should have been done by the victim.
- Endlessly seek opportunities for the victim.
- Give the victim multiple chances rather than providing negative consequences for poor work performance.

Victims

- Don't take advantage of opportunities to improve performance.
- Repeat the same offenses, like showing up late for work, repeating mistakes, and doing poor quality work.
- Blame others when problems occur.
- Let the rescuers do work for them.

Scenario

Let's take a look at how individuals act out the role of persecutor, victim, and rescuer within a work context. Glenn was talking with Curt about Beverly.

"She's late for work again, isn't she?" said Glenn, looking at his watch.

"Give her a break, man. It's only three minutes past nine," Curt said. (rescuer)

"But she starts at eight," said Glenn. (persecutor)

"Remember, she has three kids to get off to school," said Curt. (rescuer)

"Three kids. Baloney! I think she rents them." (persecutor)

Just then, Beverly walked in. She went to her desk and sat down without saying anything to the others.

"Well?" asked Glenn, "Do you know you're late?" (persecutor)

"Yes, I know I'm late. But I couldn't help it. I ran out of gas," cried Beverly. (victim)

"But we're only a half mile from your home, and the gas station is on the way," said Glenn. (persecutor)

Beverly glared at Glenn. "Well, I didn't have any money, so I had to walk home, break into my kid's piggy bank, go to the gas station, borrow a gas can, go back to the car with gas, and then drive to the gas station to put some gas in the tank." (victim)

"You shouldn't have broken into your kid's piggy bank, Beverly. Here's $10. Take it and put the money back in your child's bank," said Curt. (rescuer)

"I give up," said Glenn, rolling his eyes. He turned and began to walk away. (persecutor)

"I don't have to take that kind of talk from you! You're an idiot anyway," Beverly screamed. "I don't have to put up with this harassment. I'm leaving!" She stormed out the door, grabbing the $10 out of Curt's hand as she walked by him. (persecutor)

"What in the world was that all about?" asked Curt, befuddled by what just occurred. (victim)

"Sorry she did that to you," said Glenn, putting his arm on Curt's shoulder. "Listen, since you're out 10 bucks, I'll buy you lunch." (rescuer)

As you can see from this encounter, roles can easily shift, with the rescuer suddenly finding himself the victim and the victim shifting quickly into the persecutor role.

This scenario is played out all the time within organizations. A team is not performing as it should, so the organization recruits a new manager. The new manager walks in to the department, and wanting to be liked by the group, immediately jumps into the role of rescuer. She finds ways that she can defend everyone and take care of things for them. This provides an opportunity for the team members to step quickly into the role of victim, sharing their horror stories with her about how uncaring the organization has been. They tell her about the unreasonable expectations of the higher-ups, about the abusive language used by customers because jobs are late, and about how the sales group will promise anything to a customer to get the sale. She can't believe her ears, tells them that she understands their plight and steps into the role of their defender.

Moving on to takeover thinking requires letting go of the past. It requires recognizing when you are a participant in a drama triangle at work and consciously deciding to step out of it. If you're locked into this triangle at work, you can extricate yourself by being conscious of the roles you play and making an effort to respond to the specifics of a situation rather than lapsing into a familiar role that has nothing to do with what's going on.

☑ Takeover Rule #10: ☑

Recognize when you are a participant in a drama triangle and consciously step out of that role.

Here are some steps you can take:

- Review the list of traits for each of the three roles and determine which role you most commonly assume in a given work situation.
- If you're most commonly a persecutor, resolve to moderate your persecuting tendencies by being more empathetic. Catch yourself starting arguments with victims and chastising them, and try and understand

how your persecution is just playing into their desire to be a victim.

- If you're most commonly a rescuer, resolve to recognize that you're doing no one any good with your eagerness to defuse tensions and absolve others of responsibility. Note to yourself that your attempt to help another person is simply keeping that individual stuck in his victim role.

- If you're most commonly a victim, resolve to stop blaming others and repeating the same old mistakes. Tell yourself that you're not only hurting yourself because of the way you act, but you're hurting others who become part of the persecuting and rescuing drama.

Whether you have assumed the role of rescuer, persecutor, or victim, you invariably will feel anger about the situation you're in. It's likely you'll become angry with the other participants in the triangle. To accept the takeover mindset requires that you be willing to let go of that anger so that you can move on to a more productive relationship with them.

☑ Takeover Rule #11: ☑

Moving on to takeover thinking requires letting go of the anger you feel toward others.

The offer: How to structure it

At this point, you may not feel ready to launch a personal takeover. In trying to overcome the factors that foster victim thinking, you may find yourself worrying that you haven't fully extricated yourself from the drama triangle, that you're still influenced by media stories about victimization, that you can't let go of certain negative memories, and that you continue to participate in public executions at work. Even if this is the case, you should also recognize that you're making strides away from the victim mindset just through increased awareness of how you act.

If, however, you have decided that you would like to engage in a personal takeover, then you can start the process by making yourself an offer. Making the offer is just the start of the takeover process. Like a business takeover, it doesn't happen overnight. You may need to negotiate, revise, think about, and discuss the offer before it's successful. For now, though, the key is putting a brief statement of the offer on paper. The following will help you accomplish this task:

1. Start the offer by affirming your desire to take control of your life.
2. Note to who (or what) you gave control of your life in the past and how you are taking that power back from "them."
3. Add a sentence or two that describes your goal for this personal takeover.
4. Set a tentative date for when the takeover will take effect and the conditions for this takeover (the specific things you will do to ensure that the takeover goes smoothly).

Here is an example of a written offer:

I am going to be in charge of what happens on the job and in my career. Before, I used to feel that my boss and the organization controlled what happened to me and that I was at the mercy of fate and economic conditions. Now, I realize that I misperceived reality, and that this lack of control was mostly in my mind—all these outside forces may have an effect on what happens, but I am ultimately in charge of the path my life takes. By November 15, I intend that this personal takeover will take

)

effect if I: A) Stop thinking like a cynic all the time.
B) Start making up my own mind about what repre-
sents success rather than depending on the opin-
ions of others. C) Start living in the present rather
than harboring all these negative memories of how
others did me wrong.

The words used in this offer will vary considerably from
person to person. In some respects, what you say is less important than your willingness to say it. By putting the offer down
on paper, you're making a commitment to take control of your
life. It may take time—and effort—and you may want to change
your offer as you gain more information in the following chapters, but the simple exercise of making a formal offer will help
you move that much closer to being in control of your life.

Chapter 6

Negate Negathoughts

*❝ I've been on the treadmill of life,
but I sure ain't losin' weight."*

I T'S NOT JUST WHAT YOU BELIEVE THAT CAN STAND IN THE WAY OF A personal takeover, but the way you think. This might seem like a subtle distinction, but it's an important one. The beliefs we hold are deep-rooted and often formed in childhood. Though these beliefs influence how we think, they are beneath the surface of our thinking and more fundamental. Our thoughts are shaped by our experiences and catalyzed by the situations we face.

So unproductive thinking, or taking an unproductive view toward specific situations, can affect us every bit as much as holding negative mindsets. While it's great to be aware of the power of both to prevent takeovers, you may discover that you're able to do something about your thinking quickly and that it takes more time to address the underlying beliefs.

Now that you've made your takeover offer, you may experience all sorts of doubts about your ability to complete the offer successfully. As you read the offer you've written, you may find yourself having second thoughts: *Can I really do this? How am I going to change the way I've acted and thought after all these years? Why do I think I'm capable of controlling my life when everything that's happened to me seems random and out of my control?* These second thoughts can quickly become what I call *negathoughts*, and they catalyze and reinforce victim mindsets. This relationship is shown in the following figure.

The goal here isn't to eliminate negathoughts completely. It's the rare individual who can banish most, if not all, of his negative thinking. You had negathoughts before you made the offer to yourself, and you'll have them afterwards. What you need to recognize, however, is that they can spiral out of control and doom your efforts

to take charge of your life. Later, I'll discuss how you can convert negathoughts into takeover thinking. For now, however, the more modest objective is to manage these negathoughts and ensure that they don't overwhelm your resolve to complete your takeover.

What are negathoughts?

Negative thinking can manifest itself in a million different ways, but the negathoughts we're concerned with here are *generalizing* and *disabling* statements that totally eliminate any opportunity for success. The two italicized words are important because they separate negathoughts from very specific and non-impactive thoughts. If you're playing baseball and strike out, you might think to yourself, "That was a terrible at bat," which is not a negathought. It's a very specific thought, and it doesn't disable you because it's not suggesting that your next at bat will be equally terrible.

Negathoughts surface in our minds as concise statements that we repeat to ourselves and on which we dwell, sometimes to the point of obsession. Some examples of these nega-thoughts are:

- Nobody cares about my ideas.
- I can't speak in front of a group.
- I am terrible at math.
- This company is a dead end, but I can't leave because I am too old.
- I can't trust anyone or get too close because they will take advantage of me.
- Others don't want to talk with me because they find me boring.
- What sense does it make to offer my ideas? Nobody at this company will listen anyway.
- If I give my love to someone they are going to abandon me.
- I can't eat at a restaurant alone.
- The cards are stacked against me—no matter what I do.
- When they find out about me they will see that I am really not that good.
- It's too dangerous to go out for a walk at night.
- I bungle every job I get.
- People who work with me are lazy.
- Life sucks.

As you can see in this list, these negative thoughts are a part of many areas of our lives. They undermine much of our potential. Now, everyone has negative thoughts, and many of these are quite reasonable. For instance, a person might think, "I am behind on my project because I've been busy in meetings with other employees." In this case, the person knows why he or she is behind in the work and has alternatives. This is not a negathought. The reason negathoughts are so insidious is because they are disempowering. When someone says "I bungle every job I get," that individual is offering himself no opportunity for redemption. He is generalizing his incompetence.

Consider your reaction after you completed writing your takeover offer. Did any of the following negathoughts cross your mind?

- I am never going to be able to launch a successful takeover.
- I never reach any goals I set for myself, and this takeover will be just another example of my failure.
- I'm not assertive enough to complete this takeover.
- I always have great plans for myself but I never follow through.
- I'm incapable of controlling anything in my life.
- This takeover stuff won't work.
- I know I made a commitment with the offer, but I'm bad with commitments.

If any of these statements sound familiar, don't worry. Identifying your negathought is the first step toward changing it. Let's go through an activity that will facilitate this identification process. In the chart below, write down any negathoughts you have regarding yourself, your work, your relationships, or any other area that applies. It doesn't matter how large or small the thought may be.

Identifying Your Negathoughts

Negative or Debilitating Thoughts

Negathoughts about myself:

"I can't..."

_____

_____

_____

"I'm terrible at..."

_____

_____

_____

Negathoughts at work:

About my boss...

_____

_____

_____

About organization leadership...

_____

_____

_____

About my peers...

_____

_____

_____

About employees...

_____

_____

_____

About customers...

_____

_____

_____

Negathoughts in relationships:

About the opposite sex...

_____

_____

_____

About friendships...

_____

_____

_____

About people in general...

_____

_____

_____

Negathoughts in family:

About my parents...

_____

_____

_____

About my kids...

_____

_____

_____

Negathoughts in other contexts:

_____

_____

_____

_____

_____

As you look at your particular negathoughts, do you see a particular pattern starting to emerge? Do you think about yourself as incompetent, stupid, lazy, unimaginative, or impatient? Do you see certain themes: you're paranoid about both your customers and your family relationships; you're distrustful of a lot of different people; you're convinced that people don't like you? Whatever the theme or pattern, pay attention to it. These negathoughts are what can sabotage your personal takeover strategy. No matter how much you might want to take control of your life, these thoughts can prevent you from achieving what you want.

Vic is the owner of a small executive search firm, one that tends to do relatively well during good economic times and relatively poorly when the economy is down. Vic was convinced that he was a slave to the economy, and there was nothing he could do to change the up-and-down fortunes of his company. Look at page 111 to see what Vic's negathink analysis looked like.

In his takeover offer, Vic had written that he wanted to take back control from his "clients, the economy, and my employees." Yet when he reviewed his negathought analysis, it was clear that he didn't think himself capable of regaining this control. When Vic was honest with himself—as he was when he filled out the form—he recognized that he viewed himself as a nice, somewhat passive guy who lacked the ability to assert himself. Too many times in the past, though, Vic had resolved that he was going to be more aggressive in pursuing new clients and overcome being a slave to the economy. When a prospective client turned him down and said they had decided to hire another recruiter, Vic became discouraged and his negathoughts overwhelmed him. The same thing happened when Vic made himself a takeover offer. It only took a few days before he started doubting himself, remembering negative experiences with clients, thinking about the economy, and convincing himself that he was doing the best he could and was being foolishly optimistic to believe otherwise.

Identifying Your Negathoughts

Negative or Debilitating Thoughts

Negathoughts about myself:

"I can't..."
*Confront people; I'm incapable
of holding others accountable.*

_____

"I'm terrible at..."
*Putting my foot down and setting
firm policies and ground rules.*

_____

Negathoughts at work:

About my boss...

_____
_____
_____

About organization leadership...

_____
_____
_____

About my peers...

_____
_____
_____

About employees...

*They take advantage of every
situation and only look out for
themselves.*

About customers...

*They're only concerned about the
bottom line and have no loyalty to
me no matter how good a job I do.*

Negathoughts in relationships:

About the opposite sex...

_____
_____
_____

About friendships...

_____
_____
_____

About people in general...

_____
_____
_____

Negathoughts in family:

About my parents...

_____
_____
_____

About my kids...
They are manipulative.

_____
_____

Negathoughts in other contexts:

*I think I've been lucky to be in
this business as long as I have (8
years) but I don't believe I'm ever
going to be as successful as other
recruiters I know because I'm not
sufficiently ruthless or ambitious.*

As Vic became more conscious of his negathoughts, he found himself better able to "negate" them—or at least some of them. It was as if an alarm went off in his head when he'd take on his old victim mindset of the pawn. In the past he'd tell himself he was powerless to do anything when an employee asked for an exorbitant raise or when he had trouble completing a search on time. Now he stopped himself from thinking this way. Instead of berating himself and feeling lower than a worm looking up at a curb, Vic did something about his situation.

Having identified the negathoughts to which he was vulnerable, Vic found that he had somehow reduced their power over him. While Vic didn't magically land a big new client or turn his business around overnight, he was able to start taking some small steps in the right direction. In one instance, he was able to talk a valued employee into staying with his firm rather than taking a competitor's offer. In another instance, Vic formed an alliance with a recruiter in another field, attempting to provide them both with additional referrals. Even before Vic completed his takeover, he was seeing positive results.

Three things to think about

As you go about this step of identifying your negathoughts, keep the following three things in mind:

1. Don't put off until tomorrow what you can do today.

Even though you've started the offer process, you may be tempted to shy away from pinpointing your cynical, pessimistic, and otherwise negative thoughts. You might think to yourself, *I can do this later in the process; I can wait until I've done more exercises and gathered more information before I really address these thoughts.* Don't postpone this important task. It takes some time to turn victim thinking into takeover thinking, and the sooner you start, the better. Recognize that these negathoughts are what hold you back and give rise to the different types of victim mindsets. As an incentive to start negating your negathoughts now, memorize this truism:

☑ Takeover Rule #12: ☑

Each negathought you replace with a positive alternative will have a dramatically positive effect on your future.

**2. Be aware that you hold your
negathoughts near and dear to your heart.**

Negathoughts are powerful, even though they may leave us powerless. If you underestimate the hold they have on your thinking, you may not be able to muster the willpower necessary to let them go. Clarissa, for instance, had spent years thinking that organizations were Darwinian places where only the strongest survived; she was certain that if she showed any vulnerability to her fellow workers, they would use it against her. As a result, she went about her work in a cold and somewhat ruthless manner. These negathoughts worked against her, especially as her company became more relationship-driven. Clarissa, however, had just about brainwashed herself into believing that the moment she became open and honest was the moment that would spell her doom in the company. She took an odd sort of comfort in this thought, viewing it as what protected her from those politically minded foes who wanted to push her aside. In fact, these thoughts were what held Clarissa back. Her inability to form strong, open relationships made her a poor fit in an increasingly team-oriented environment. Logically, you would think that Clarissa would have recognized this fact and released her negathoughts. Their hold on her, however, was sufficient to make this quite a difficult task to accomplish. Therefore, accept that you're going to have to work hard at managing your negathoughts. It's not simply a matter of writing your takeover statement and watching all your negative thoughts disappear. It takes perseverance and commitment just to identify them. Recognize that you have to focus on fighting your negathoughts and that it's going to take a period of time before you have them under control. The good news is that when you have them under control, you benefit in many ways, and this will reinforce your resolve.

3. Your experiences can keep your negathoughts locked in place.

Changing these negathoughts means changing the way you think. As you start identifying them and learn to keep them at bay, you may become "suspicious" of how your thinking is changing. After all, you've been negathinking your way through life for years. The new thought patterns emerging in your mind may feel unfamiliar and even strange. You may question the takeover process and whether you're trying to be someone you're not.

This is especially true if you've been burned in the past. Perhaps you were treated unfairly by bosses or organizations. Perhaps you were passed over for a deserved promotion or you experienced a business failure because your partner didn't pull his weight. All these negative experiences may make your negathoughts seem like a "realistic" way to think. While some people might treat you unfairly or act in hurtful ways toward you, don't let these instances dictate your mindset. In most cases, our past experiences are largely positive, but it's the relatively few negative events that come to dominate our thinking and make us feel that we're naive or weird to think in positive ways.

Remind yourself that the unpleasant and unfair events that took place in your past aren't indicative of what will take place in the future.

A leap of faith

As you move through the takeover process, you're going to be reminded of incidents from your past that challenge your belief that you are capable of personal empowerment. While I'll try to provide examples and exercises to demonstrate that these were isolated incidents and that your ability to carve your own path is in your hands and your hands alone, you're going to need to take a leap of faith. You need to believe that success and fulfillment are within your grasp and that no person or event can prevent you from achieving these things.

To a certain extent, you've already made this leap of faith by picking up this book. In doing so, you made a statement that you want to either change yourself or help someone else to change (and if it's the latter, you have to model this new way of thinking). Now you need to pay off that first commitment by taking the steps to move beyond negathought. A world is out there waiting to unfold for you—a world that may be very different from the one you presently know. The exciting thing is, when you allow yourself to be able to experience it, it will be there. The beneficial relationships, the promising jobs, and the business opportunities will all be there if you only allow them to be there. If you take the leap of faith and believe that all these things are possible for you, your world will begin to change in wonderful and rewarding ways.

Chapter 7

The Takeover Mindset: Finding Your Personal Power

❝❝ *I've been down a long time,
but now it's time to get up."*

One of the hallmarks of a corporate takeover is that the acquiring group gains decision-making power. This is critical, in that they can put their vision and strategy into practice rather than depend on others for their success. It's tremendously frustrating to have this vision and strategy and not be able to implement it. Corporate takeovers often have their origin in the acquiring group's frustration with a company's strategy and their belief that if they gain control, they can shift the strategy in a much more profitable direction.

Having made an offer and identified your negathoughts, you're now ready to shift your thinking in a more profitable direction. Takeover thinking means you're in charge of making decisions and determining your fate. Takeover thinking is finding your personal power. If this sounds like what you want, terrific. Be aware, however, that you're not going to shift from a victim mindset to a takeover mindset overnight. Your goal here is to start moving your thinking in a new direction. Subsequent chapters will help you to convert your thinking completely.

Let's start out by examining what takeover thinking looks like, especially in contrast to victim thinking.

There are no conditions in this deal

Why do you want to become a top executive of your company, achieve great wealth, or even find the love of your life? Because you, like many of us, want to achieve a sense of well-being. True empowerment, true success, comes about as a result of a genuine sense of well-being; but it is a misleading paradox because the search for material accomplishment or material gain, as an attempt to achieve an internal sense of well being, often accomplishes the opposite. The person who links well-being to accomplishment has fallen prey to conditional thinking. It amounts to success built upon conditions, and when you set conditions for your own sense of personal success, you end up on a constant treadmill. You'll find yourself constantly striving for that next goal, that next possession, finding that each time you achieve it, the euphoria you expected just isn't there. You end up with a flat feeling inside, trying to figure out what it is you must achieve to be able to feel okay about yourself and about the world. The treadmill involves constantly trying to acquire more toys, more possessions, and more milestones. If these conditions aren't met, you feel as if you've failed. In reality, success based upon material possessions or certain accomplishments ends up being quite shallow.

☑ Takeover Rule #13: ☑

True empowerment, true success, comes about
as a result of a genuine sense of well-being. The search
for material accomplishment or material gains,
as an attempt to achieve well-being,
often accomplishes the opposite.

When you become a takeover thinker, on the other hand, you begin to grasp the secret of well-being: It comes about solely as a result of your view of reality—and nothing more. It is not based on being a multimillionaire; it is not based on being a famous movie star. It is merely based on being comfortable with yourself, on accepting yourself, and choosing to define your own well-being as a result of just being alive and able to experience life on a daily basis. You might not have a prestigious job, drive an expensive car, or possess the latest personal digital assistant, yet you will lead a happier, more fulfilling life if you possess this internal sense of well-being.

People who have the takeover mindset gain this sense of well-being because they see themselves as having control over the environment, they readily accept accountability, and they choose to be optimistic about the events taking place around them. The takeover thinker takes an optimistic view toward the world, rather than an unproductive mindset and a cynical view. He or she views people as basically good and is confident and trusting of others. Let's look at an example.

Scenario

Phillip is orienting a new group of management trainees to his firm.

"Welcome, everyone, to Betty's Logistics, one of the most advanced software-solution firms in the market today. Betty seized upon an opportunity to form this organization when the governor of our state had a sewage problem that was not being dealt with."

There are smiles from everyone around the room as each person thinks about what a good decision this was to join Betty's Logistics.

"Here is Betty now," says Phillip, as Betty walks into the room and sits at the table with the new recruits. "As I was saying, Betty seized a real opportunity and we haven't stopped growing since. You can never be fast enough in this market. Remember the dinosaurs. They didn't adapt so they're extinct today."

"Of course, dinosaurs had brains the size of a pea," suggests a new recruit.

"You're right," replies Phillip, "we have the capability to adapt more readily, maybe because our brains are not the size of a pea."

"I like peas," says one of the other new recruits.

Nervous looks appear around the room. Betty makes a mental note to herself, *Rethink current recruiting procedures.*

"While a lot of others were seeing the sewers as half-empty, we were seeing them as half-full," says Betty. "They were thinking the governor just wanted a scapegoat for his sewage problem, but we saw a real opportunity if we could satisfy him."

"Yeah, I was one of them," continued Phillip, "but Betty showed me the value of co-, co-...."

"Come on Phillip. You can say it."

"Co-...collaboration."

In the preceding dialogue, one can see an optimistic tone. Betty took a sewage problem, and because she didn't have a glass half-empty mindset, she turned it into a positive opportunity. Phillip moved from his own win-lose thinking—seeing everyone else as a competitor—to seeing the upside of collaboration.

It is important to make the distinction of how differently the victim and the takeover thinker view the world and view others. Let's assume that you have a takeover mindset and one of your coworkers, Jim, has a victim mindset—he's a classic cynic.

Mark, a new hire, joins your team, and you are excited to have him on the team because he brings a wealth of new experiences and expertise—he used to work at one of your company's competitors, and you're anxious to learn about his old company's policies and practices. When you meet Mark, you immediately ask him out to lunch and talk freely about the good things within your company as well as the bad. You trust him, and so you're perfectly willing to be open about your perspective on the organization.

When you tell Jim about your lunch with Mark, however, he thinks you're naive. He says Mark might turn around and tell his former boss about your company's weaknesses. He also says that he's not interested in learning about the competitor's practices because "they're even more screwed up than we are." Jim says that when he was introduced to Mark, he kept their exchange to a few innocuous words. Jim adds that he views Mark as one more rival for the prized opening in the company's New York office and that he's sure that Mark views him in the same light. "I trust him about as much as I trust all the other people on our team, which is to say, not at all," Jim says.

Like many cynics, Jim uses his cynicism as a shield. He is afraid of looking bad, convinced that if he trusts Mark, Mark will betray that trust and make him look like a fool. The take-over mentality, however, suggests that somebody else cannot make you look foolish. You would be disappointed if Mark shared your conversation with other people in his former company, but you would also recognize that you spoke the truth as you saw it and that Mark merely communicated this truth to other people. At worst, Mark would be the one who looks foolish, having repeated a private conversation without considering the ramifications.

With his victim mindset, however, Jim looks at all this quite differently. Even the slightest chance that he might be made to look foolish makes him anxious. This view is an example of the external locus of control, based on the belief that events or people around us become a reflection on us and can cause us to appear a certain way to others. It's a focus more on an external image than an inner self-confidence. Jim's victim mindset also causes him to see the universe as one of scarcity, so he has to compete with others for dwindling resources. This is as opposed to the takeover mindset, where you see a world of abundance.

The takeover mindset is the polar opposite of the victim mindset, yet you can begin acquiring the takeover mindset one piece at a time. Try the following exercise in order to start shifting your thinking from victim to takeover. Begin by making a check mark next to any of the following work behaviors that might be characteristic of you:

- ☐ Treating new members of your work team or group with suspicion.
- ☐ Talking cynically or fatalistically about your future with the company.
- ☐ Refusing to take on challenging work assignments, preferring easy, routine tasks where there's less likelihood of things going wrong.
- ☐ Refusing to be open and honest with coworkers, bosses, or direct reports because you fear your honesty will get you in trouble.
- ☐ Spending a great deal of time gossiping with fellow employees about who's going to be let go and other worst-case scenarios.
- ☐ Telling customers or clients what they want to hear rather than the truth because you fear that the truth will cause problems.
- ☐ Ignoring or being rude to people in the organization who you consider unimportant to your career or "beneath" you.
- ☐ Taking sole credit rather than sharing credit when your team was responsible for a successful project.
- ☐ Creating elaborate strategies to cover yourself in case something goes wrong.

Pick just one of the checked items from the list and write a paragraph describing the thinking behind this action. Put down your rationale for behaving this particular way. Do you see any of your negathoughts surfacing? Are they indicative of any of the victim mindset types previously delineated? Does your thinking fly in the face of your takeover statement?

If so, make a week-long commitment to try and change this thinking relative to the particular action you targeted. For instance, if you checked "Telling customers or clients what they want to hear…" and the rationale behind this action was that you're convinced they'll complain to your boss about you if you level with them, change your thinking in the following way: *Though a customer or client might be angry with me if I tell them bad news or expose a problem they didn't know existed, if they're reasonable people, they'll appreciate my honesty and trust me more because of it. I have the responsibility for making sure I communicate bad news in a responsible way— that I don't blow things out of proportion or communicate in a panicked way if a panic truly doesn't exist. Assuming I have communicated a problem reasonably, if a customer becomes furious with me for being honest and complains about me, then they're not a good customer to have, and I'm better off without them.*

Be resolute; don't give in to victim thinking in this one area for the entire week. At the end of the week, evaluate how this new mode of thinking impacted your actions. If you're pleased with the results—or even if you're uncertain—extend this thinking one more week and evaluate again. The odds are that you'll find this taste of takeover thinking to your liking and adopt it permanently.

Traits of the two types of mindset

The following chart clearly differentiates takeover from victim thinking:

Contrasting the Takeover Mindset
From the Victim Mindset

THE VICTIM MINDSET	THE TAKEOVER MINDSET
The cynic • Takes a cynical view toward the world. • Focuses on survival and sees self against the world. • Questions motives and is suspicious of others.	*The optimist* • Takes an optimistic view toward the world. • Views people as basically good. • Displays confidence in self and is trusting of others.
The win-lose individual • Sees a world of scarcity. • Competes with coworkers for people and resources. • Addresses problems or issues in an adversarial way.	*The believer in win-win* • Sees a universe of abundance, so there is enough for everyone. • Cooperates and collaborates with coworkers. • Sees others as partners and friends instead of adversaries.
The pawn • Possesses an external locus of control, seeing control outside of self, thus resulting in statements like, "You're the reason I'm this way." • Displays a "poor me" attitude. • Attributes events to fate, and responds with statements like, "Why try? It wouldn't be approved anyway."	*The individual who sees options* • Possesses an internal locus of control, believing events are not totally out of own control. • Feels he or she has control over own destiny. • Believes there are always options in every difficult situation.
The glass half-empty individual • Chooses to see the negative side of any situation. • Finds it difficult to get beyond the problem, so rarely finds a solution. • Focuses on what won't work instead of what will work.	*The glass half-full individual* • Chooses to see the positive side of any situation. • Doesn't get overwhelmed by the problem and often sees opportunity in adversity. • Focuses on what will work instead of what won't work.
The blame-shifter • Avoids responsibility.	*The self-responsible individual* • Shows willingness to assume responsibility and accountability, often beyond the scope of immediate position.

Contrasting the Takeover Mindset From the Victim Mindset, *cont'd*

THE VICTIM MINDSET	THE TAKEOVER MINDSET
The blame-shifter • Shifts the blame to others when problems arise. • Seeks scapegoats when things go wrong.	*The self-responsible individual* • Takes the initiative to correct problems. • Seeks solutions instead of placing blame.
The chronic complainer • Displays an unwillingness to take charge or lead efforts. • Complains continually, without providing solutions. • Sows negativity in the organization and helps breed discontent.	*The rarely complaining individual* • Leads efforts to fix problems rather than complaining about them. • Sees complaining as an unproductive endeavor. • Maintains a realistic perspective of organizational life and doesn't expect everything to be perfect.
The work-avoider • Sees work as necessary evil. • Spends large amounts of time on personal or social activities instead of the work itself. • Fails to volunteer to do anything beyond the assigned tasks.	*The individual to whom work is critical* • Sees work as an important part of life. • Focuses on getting results instead of being caught up in activities. • Challenges self to higher levels of accomplishment.
The bored individual • Shows little initiative in keeping self-interested. • Expects to be entertained. • Utilizes all personal, vacation, and sick time available and tries to find more.	*The actively engaged individual* • Shows high level of interest in building relationships. • Finds ways to challenge self and keep work interesting. • Takes responsibility for own level of happiness and sense of satisfaction with work.
The critic • Criticizes other people and discounts their efforts. • Sees self as being better than everyone else. • Makes openly critical comments about the organization.	*The self-critic* • Accepts personal accountability when a problem occurs, and attempts to determine what he or she could have done to prevent it. • Sees the value in coworkers. • Focuses continually on self-improvement.

Let's look at some of these traits in more depth and the corresponding takeover-friendly actions you can take.

Takeover thinkers see a world that can potentially satisfy everyone's needs. If we believe in this world of abundance, we can engage in win/win, because others do not have to get more at our expense. If each of us can win, then we can cooperate with and root for others. Takeover thinkers view others as partners rather than adversaries. They seek the opportunity to join with others to achieve mutual goals, where everyone benefits.

Nelson Mandela, then President of South Africa, demonstrated takeover thinking when he was to attend an international economic forum in Switzerland in February of 1997. He appointed Chief Mangosuthu Buthelezi acting President while he was away. Chief Buthelezi was the leader of the Inkatha Freedom Party and the archrival to Mandela. At first, Senate members snickered because they thought Mandela was kidding. They assumed no one would appoint, even for such a short trip, the person who was his political opponent. Mandela, though, stopped the snickering by saying that Mr. Buthelezi was both experienced and competent to stand in for him. Chief Buthelezi was in awe and responded that he would not do anything to destroy that trust. This demonstration of takeover thinking on the part of President Mandela is particularly profound in light of the fact that Mandela's party, the African National Congress, and Buthelezi's party, the Inkatha Freedom Party, had engaged in many years of bloody fighting with each other.

Fate is not part of the takeover thinker's mindset. Fate is based on the external locus of control—the idea that control lies outside of us. Takeover thinkers have an internal locus of control, viewing destiny as something within their own grasp. They realize they will be able to control their future. This doesn't mean that nothing bad will ever happen to them—life is life, and sometimes it can be tough. We all are going to face adversity. The difference is that, instead of shrugging their shoulders and attributing everything to fate, takeover thinkers see themselves as having options. If they believe that they can generate options for change, they will always have a way out of a difficult situation.

☑ Takeover Rule #14: ☑

If you believe you have options, there will always be a way out of even the most difficult situation.

Classic entrepreneurs embody this way of thinking. Some of our most successful entrepreneurs have a history of failure. Bankruptcy and public failure is often part of their resume. It's very easy to give up when these failures occur, but the entrepreneurial spirit drives people to explore other options and opportunities. They are convinced that they can succeed if they just keep trying new projects. They view failure as an isolated occurrence rather than a predictor of the future, allowing them to let go of even the worst disasters and start over.

What's disturbing is that, as a nation, we may be losing some of our takeover mentality and slipping into victim mindsets. A popular business magazine did a story on successful, self-made millionaires in the United States today. They found that a surprising number of successful entrepreneurs came from the former Soviet Union. Why? They concluded that conditions were so tough in the Soviet Union, these entrepreneurs could handle the setbacks they encountered in the United States, while many American-born business people were more likely to give up during hard times.

People with the takeover mindset are self-responsible. They seek solutions instead of placing blame. They take the initiative to solve problems, enabling them to move forward. They tend to be risk takers, willing to stand out in front, and they tend to be results-oriented. They see bad times as a normal part of life and not something that's permanently disabling. Admittedly, this part of the takeover mindset can be challenging to acquire. To help you, I'd like to share a story and then an exercise.

Lou was a partner in a consulting firm that at one time had almost 100 employees and was growing like crazy. It seemed like the sky was the limit because the firm had established a niche and enjoyed a great reputation in their industry. However, one of Lou's partners, Harry, became bored with the business (though not with the income it generated). At one time, Harry had been a rainmaker, bringing in new clients regularly. But he developed other interests and began spending less time at the firm. Even when he was there, he just seemed to be going through the motions. Then the firm was hit by a lawsuit, a number of clients departed abruptly, and in a matter of a few months, the firm went from being a market leader to bankruptcy.

Though Lou was upset with this turn of events—he lost a significant amount of money and felt betrayed by his partner—he didn't rail at the heavens and blame fate. Nor did he become involved in the acrimonious debate raging among the firm's partners as to who was at fault for the financial mess. Instead, he jumped back into the entrepreneurial waters immediately after the firm disbanded. Lou helped his daughter start an Internet-related business. She was very bright and had this idea that made sense to him. She suggested that there might be a market for a company that could design Websites for large corporations. Lou was excited about the opportunity to work with his daughter, and he figured his business sense, combined with her high-tech savvy, might allow them to build a profitable business. Not only did they build a profitable business, but they sold it to a large high tech conglomerate for almost $20 million, two years after they started it.

Lou could have easily been wary of a new business venture; he could have cautioned his daughter about all the risks involved in starting a company and suggested that she would be better off working for someone else first. He could have applied for a job with another company himself and been hired in a second. Instead, he gave himself decision-making authority rather than ceding it to fate. He determined that just because something went wrong with his previous business, it didn't mean something would go wrong with his next business. He decided that partnering with his daughter was something he really wanted to do and refused to allow fear or pessimism to dictate his decision.

Think of a failure you've experienced in your work life. Perhaps you were part of a business that went under. Perhaps you were fired from a good job. Perhaps you failed to get a job you applied for. Whatever it was, answer the following questions related to the failure:

1. Were you reluctant to put yourself in a similar position after this failure because you feared history would repeat itself?

2. Did you blame someone or something for the failure (fate, another person, the economy, etc.)?

3. Did you beat yourself up over the failure, telling yourself you were stupid and no good at your job or your business?

4. Even if this failure occurred years ago, are you still reluctant to put yourself in a similar position?

If you answered yes to any of these questions, recognize that you have the capacity to rebound from failure like Lou or any of the classic entrepreneurs throughout history. Therefore, the next time you fail at something, keep the following truisms in mind:

- One failure does not automatically lead to another.
- Failure is an opportunity to learn and avoid making the same mistakes twice.
- Your mindset is the most important factor in your success or failure, far more important than things such as the economy, luck, and other people.

Repeating these truisms to yourself will help you start thinking like a takeover maven rather than a pawn, cynic, or loser.

☑ Takeover Rule #15: ☑

Your mindset is the most important factor in your success or failure—far more important.

You only have so much time in this life. In essence, time is your currency. You can spend that time productively or unproductively. If you hold a takeover mindset, you won't likely dwell on your problems or shortcomings. Instead, when problems arise, as they sometimes will, you'll focus on overcoming them and moving on.

If you're a victim, on the other hand, you'll more likely become stuck. Investing your energy in finding fault and absolving yourself of responsibility will leave you precious little time or inclination to seek solutions.

At some point, perhaps someone you admired took ownership of a problem. She stood up and said, "This was my fault," and didn't offer excuses or attempt to assign blame. Clearly and cleanly, she took full responsibility and the consequences that came with it. It may have been that she was reprimanded or even fired for this action. If she was a business owner, she may have lost customers. If she was the CEO of a public company, she may have taken heat from the media. But I would bet anything that her willingness to assume responsibility allowed her to succeed later on; that it marked her as a leader in the minds of many and earned her a significant amount of trust.

Takeover thinkers also tend to be results-oriented. One of the biggest differences between truly successful people and unsuccessful people is that the successful people focus on results instead of activities. They identify those activities that yield the greatest results and they invest heavily in them. They spend their time in meaningful ways, with accomplishment in mind.

Take a piece of paper and divide it with a vertical line. Title the left column "Results" and the right column "Activities." Look at your calendar or computer log for the previous Wednesday and make a list of what you did that was an activity and what you did that was designed to obtain specific results. If you're like most people who have not yet accomplished a takeover, you'll be alarmed to find the activities column filled and the results column mostly blank. You'll see that you spent the day returning mundane phone calls, sending routine e-mails, and doing a lot of paperwork. You did a lot, but you didn't accomplish much. The takeover mentality looks for activities that achieve meaningful results. While there are always some mundane tasks that need to be done, results shouldn't get downplayed because of them.

After working many years with both victims and those who display the takeover mindset, I came to realize that people with takeover mindsets value work. For them, work is an avocation instead of merely a job. As an avocation, work demands a commitment. Unlike victim mindsets, the takeover mentality encourages them to make an emotional as well as an intellectual investment in what's being done for a living. They aren't working for the money or the prestige or the perks. Instead, work becomes an essential part of who they are, and they naturally want to make a commitment to it. This commitment, in turn, helps them bring tremendous energy to the job. They are excited about coming to work and eager for the challenges it brings.

It shouldn't come as any surprise that commitment and energy translate into success. By contrast, you can probably form a mental picture of a bored employee arriving for work in the morning. Bedraggled, mentally dull, and sleepy-eyed, he trudges into the office and slogs through tasks, taking twice as long to do them as necessary and not doing them with any creativity or thoroughness. This isn't to say that a takeover mentality guarantees that you'll always be excited about what you're doing, but it certainly predisposes you to go about your tasks with energy and purpose.

I also want to emphasize one other important difference between takeover and victim mindsets that has been implied, though not specifically stated. The victim mentality is one that tends to hold others back; they see their own success as inversely proportional to the success of others. It's almost as if there is only so much success to go around, and they want to grab theirs before other people grab it. Takeover thinkers are optimistic and want others to do well; they believe that their coworkers can be successful and want to lift them to that success. They want to do well for the greater good of their group, their team, and their organization.

People with the takeover mindset do not always follow the rules. They determine what makes sense, and if something doesn't, their takeover thinking requires that they consider taking a risk to do the right thing. In 1944, an illegal basketball game was played between two college teams in Durham, North Carolina. The game was between the Eagles from the North Carolina College for Negroes (now North Carolina Central University) and a group of players from Duke University. At that time, the N.C.A.A. did not allow African-American universities to participate in the championship, yet North Carolina

College had a team that could win that year. The Duke players, though, secretly went to North Carolina College, and with no one in attendance, played against them. At the end of this game—which violated the Jim Crow laws—the score was Eagles 88: Visitors 44. Then the teams played a second game, but this time they mixed their squads. This was an even greater violation of the laws. If these players had been caught, they all would have been in serious trouble. But even with possible punishment, they were not afraid to rise above the social mores at the time and play basketball. Afterward, both teams quietly retreated to the residence hall and just talked. The game had a huge impact on the views of both teams and left an indelibly positive mark on each player.

This was an example of takeover thinking, of the innate desire for others to succeed. Victim thinkers would never have participated in the game because there was no clear individual reward; they would have imagined a million worst-case scenarios and bowed out. They would not have taken the risk that these players assumed back in 1944.

Identifying your takeover vs. victim traits

As I've emphasized before, awareness is crucial to a successful takeover, and one exercise that will help you develop this awareness involves assessing the takeover traits versus the victim traits you possess. Recognize that you're going to have a mixture of traits from both columns, and that what's important, right now, is to make these traits conscious. The only way you're going to stop thinking like a victim is by starting to know *how* you think like a victim.

Go back to the chart (p. 124) comparing the victim mindset with the takeover mindset. Take a look at the chart and check off each trait that applies to you. You should have check marks on both sides of the chart. (If you find you only have check marks on the takeover mindset side, you are probably not being honest with yourself—try to be more objective). Count the number of checks you have on each side. Do you have more checks on the victim side or on the takeover side?

Checks on both sides mean that you are not all of a victim mindset, nor are you all of a takeover mindset. The difference between a victim and takeover mindset is that people who are more predominately a victim will likely have more checks on the victim side. Those who are more of the takeover mindset will have more checks on the takeover side.

You might find an interesting phenomenon when you look at the checks you have made. For instance, you might see that you behave more self-empowered at work but behave more like a victim in your personal life.

Making a consistent effort to be aware of your victim traits will help you make the transition to your personal takeover; these traits will turn into red flags that will warn you when your victim mindset emerges. When you raise your level of awareness, you automatically start making subtle changes in how you act.

In fact, subtle changes should be an initial takeover goal. Your success is merely a matter of frequency. You only have to change the frequency with which you display the traits of a takeover mindset to move toward a personal takeover. If you can just use the takeover traits a little more and the victim traits a little less, you can make a major difference in your life.

There's a very thin line between successful people and unsuccessful ones; crossing over to the successful side requires only a subtle evolution in mindset. Though I don't expect you to make a complete shift here—that's what the rest of the takeover process is about—you can start by increasing your awareness of when you approach situations as a victim, and then you can begin changing that approach whenever you recognize it.

This idea of frequency is a critical and powerful element of moving from victim mindset to personal takeover. Believe it or not, the differences between victims and those who have achieved a personal takeover are not huge differences. Surprisingly, subtle changes in your mindset and the resulting behaviors will yield dramatic progress toward a personal takeover. This leads to takeover rule #16.

☑ Takeover Rule #16: ☑

If you wish to achieve a personal takeover and become more self-empowered, merely increase the frequency with which you act self-empowered.

Let's look at takeover rule #16 in action. Tonya is a manager within a manufacturing company. One of her employees, Walt, is a chronic complainer. Walt never has anything positive to say. He whines about everything. When a problem arises, he is the first to start pointing fingers and stirring things up instead of trying to find a solution. He never takes the lead in trying to solve a problem, because he doesn't want to be too visible or too much at risk.

Recently, Walt suddenly changed. One day he walked into her office and said, "Sorry to bother you, Tonya, but we just had a customer complaint. The store never received the shipment we were supposed to get to them three weeks ago. But I think I know what happened. Sammy and I have been talking. We think the shipping slip got misplaced during the big snowstorm. What I'd like to do is this. I found the order on the computer, and Sammy and I have already filled it. I can drive it over there right now. Then Sammy and I want to work out a few ideas we have that we think will prevent misplaced orders in the future. We want to bring these ideas to you and see what you think, okay?"

What would go through your mind in this situation? Would you think, *Has Walt suddenly become possessed?* That's exactly what Tonya thought. Remember, he had done nothing but whine in the past. She was very skeptical at first. But he followed through and did exactly what he said he would do. If you were Tonya, wouldn't you feel great about him? And what if the next time an incident occurred, Walt took the lead in trying to correct the situation again? Can you see how rapidly your view of him might shift?

Like Walt, we're all capable of shifting our mindsets, and we really don't have to do that much to shift them. Though Walt's behavior appears to have undergone a 180-degree change, the change in his mindset was much less dramatic.

It started on a bet with Sammy, his fellow worker. Let's hear Walt tell the story:

Scenario

I was complaining about something a few months ago, I don't even remember what, but Sammy came up to me and basically said, "I'm sick of your grumbling. All you do is complain. You never try to fix things." I told him he didn't know what he was talking about, but then he said, "Okay, give me one example of when you took the lead in solving a problem around here." Well, he had me, and I knew it.

I don't like to be challenged that way, so I didn't talk with Sammy for at least a month, unless I had to. Then one day last week we were both at the coffee machine and he said, "So how long are you going to punish me for telling you that you complain too much?" I began to respond by making a face of surprise and asking him, "What do you mean?" but I couldn't finish it without laughing. We both knew what I was doing. So I just said, "I'm mad at you." He suggested we let bygones be bygones, for the sake of our relationship, but that the next time a problem occurred, he bet I wouldn't take the lead in fixing it. I asked him, "How much?" He said he'd buy my lunch if I took the lead or I'd have to buy his if I didn't.

Well, don't you know that two days later we got that customer complaint. I tried to lay low, but around the corner comes Sammy with a big grin on his face. I said I'd do it, but he needed to help me. Well, he did, and we solved it together, but he made me go to Tonya. Actually, I got mentioned in the company newsletter for solving the problem, and besides getting lunch from Sammy, Tonya gave me a $100 spot reward. Well, now I'm looking for problems to solve, just to show Sammy and the rest of them that they were wrong about me.

Walt just accepted the idea that he would be more successful by solving problems than by complaining about them. Eventually he realized that he was responsible for what happened to him at work and that the victim notion that others were to blame was nonsense. He increased the frequency with which he employed a takeover trait—seeking solutions instead of shifting blame—and significant changes occurred.

Too often, we underestimate the impact a shift in our thoughts can have. In part, this is because we assume others have decision-making authority over us, never really defining who these "others" are. We figure that some indefinite collection of people, luck, and fate determines what we do with our lives and where we go in organizations and careers. When we shift this view—when we realize that the decision-making authority rests within us—it can have an enormously positive impact on our actions.

As you work at moving yourself toward a takeover mindset, keep the following adage and story in mind:

> *Fate is what life gives me;*
> *destiny is what I choose to do with it.*

The story involves two shoe salesmen who were sent to the Australian outback in the early 1900s. After considerable time there, one telegraphed back to the main office, "No opportunity here. Natives don't wear shoes." The other telegraphed back the same day, "Great opportunities here. Natives don't wear shoes." It's not difficult to guess which of these two salesmen had the best chance of being successful.

If you can shift your thinking from, "no opportunities here" to, "great opportunities here," you're well on your way to a personal takeover.

Chapter 8

Success Is a Matter of Choice

" " *My garden of life was full of weeds,*
but then I met a rose. "

Success is a matter of choice. Those who feel most successful and have a sense of well-being typically have chosen to be that way. We make choices regarding our reality. We choose our mindsets about the nature of reality. We choose how we are going to interpret the data we receive every day, to either confirm or challenge our reality. We choose our activities and choose our behaviors. We can choose to engage in activities that lead us to accomplishment, or we can choose those activities that work against it. We can decide to spend our time productively, or we can decide to spend it unproductively.

In our interactions with others, we can choose to act in ways that will cause people to be attracted to us, or we can choose to act in ways that would repel others. The choice is ours to make. Choice is an important piece of the takeover mindset. Choices provide us with options, but also provide us with the reality that there are trade-offs. You can have anything you want. You just can't have *everything* you want, unless your wants are pretty finite.

This is an important notion, because many of us see ourselves as having fallen short, often as a result of comparing ourselves with others. With very few exceptions, almost every one of us could achieve just about anything we want if we were willing to make the trade-offs to get it. For instance, let's say you want to get a plane and learn how to fly. No matter what job you hold presently, you could make the trade-offs that would eventually get you that plane. Now, it might take your entire life to achieve this, but you would be able to acquire it—if that is what is important to you.

Don't believe me? Let's look at a real-life example. You could buy a used, four-passenger plane today, in flying condition, for between $50,000 and $80,000. Let's say you currently rent an apartment for $1,000 per month and spend $200 per month dining out. You could move to an apartment for $500 per month and no longer go to restaurants. This would save you $8,400 per year. In six years you would have saved just over $50,000.

After moving from your $1,000 apartment to a $500 apartment, you're probably going to decide to spend the majority of your time in the plane, so maybe you don't want to make a sacrifice quite so big. You could, instead, choose to participate in a timeshare plane ownership, where you have use of the plane for a certain number of hours in a year. The point is, no matter what your level of income, you could give up some other things to get that plane.

Grasping this notion of choice is tremendously empowering. Ultimately, it helps you develop self-responsibility, a trait of a takeover mindset. In fact, the idea of choice is a cornerstone of takeover thinking. If you accept the idea that you are in control of the choices you make, then you can also accept the responsibility for not always making choices that take you in the right direction. If you're going to be a takeover thinker, you're going to take responsibility for the choices you make, no matter how they turn out.

☑ Takeover Rule #17: ☑

Acquiring the takeover mindset requires accepting responsibility for the choices you make, no matter how they may turn out.

Scenario

Marie had worked for the same retail organization for most of her life, convinced she had no other options.

"At one time," Marie reminisces, "I thought I had a real future there. But the hours required to get to the top were more than I was willing to give. I stayed there for 35 years. I was in a high-level support function, but it was just that—support. I found myself getting very negative about the organization, because I knew I wasn't going to get any higher. I felt stuck. I remember thinking, *I'll be stuck in this support role the rest of my life, because they won't promote me and I can't leave.*

Then one day it hit me. *I hate this job*, I thought. *But I'm the one who is keeping me here. No one has me chained to this company.* I began waiting for an early retirement option, thinking I would grab that up, but then I realized it might never come. So, I called Human Resources and found that my current pension would provide me with about 50 percent of what I figured I'd need to live on after 65. Then I told myself again how miserable I was in my current job and realized I'd be willing to work until 70 if I could find a job I really liked doing. So I quit. I joined this little company not far from my home, and I love every minute of what I do today."

Marie used the technique of rethinking her negathoughts to capitalize on her power of choice. Remember that nega-thoughts are those thoughts that totally disempower us, because they provide no sense of control over a situation and no options for getting out. Marie took a situation where she seemed stuck and rewrote the situation in her mind to show that she really had some choice in this matter.

Rethinking negathoughts is something you can do in any situation where you feel you have no choice. It's particularly useful in work situations. For example, let's assume that you believe that your boss doesn't trust you. Your boss may have excluded you from a new team or asked you to not deal with a particular customer, so you have concluded it's because he doesn't trust you.

There certainly can be a situation where a boss doesn't trust a subordinate. But think about this for a moment. Where is the power in this thought? As long as you believe that your boss doesn't trust you, you have given all of your power to your boss. The question to ask yourself is, *Is this really the case?* For instance, you might overreact to being questioned by your boss; he has been asking you a lot of probing ques-tions about how you interacted with a former customer who recently signed on with your company's competitor. As he questions you, you start thinking, *He must be convinced that I've done something wrong, that's why he won't let me work with our new customer. He doesn't trust me because he believes I screwed up in the past, and there's nothing I can do about it now, so I'm pretty much stuck.*

It's also possible, however, that you (like many people) become oversensitive when your boss starts asking tough questions about a problematic situation. I have seen many people who are overly sensitive to any type of questioning do this. If this is the case, your negathought might be re-worded to state, *I overreact to questioning from my boss.* The difference in this statement, as compared to your boss not trusting you, is that you have now identified a problem you can change. In rewriting your negathought, you have given yourself the power to change it. Your overreaction to questioning is something that can be changed by you, whereas your boss's lack of trust in you is something over which you would have no power whatsoever. Suddenly, you have all sorts of options that you wouldn't have if you were convinced your boss didn't trust you.

Let's take another example. Assume that your negathought is, *I'm not creative*. Again, as long as you make a blanket statement like *I'm not creative*, you have robbed yourself of choice. It's highly unlikely that you'll attempt to do anything about it. You're unlikely to participate in brainstorming sessions, fearful that others will judge you to be a drag on the team. If you have your eyes on a particular position at work, but you find it requires creativity, you're likely to shy away from it. You have taken a stand, and unfortunately, that stand is going to keep you right where you are. It's no different than stating, "I can't ice skate." This may be true, but odds are you could ice skate if you ever chose to take skating lessons, to buy the right size skates, and learn to tie the laces appropriately. The same applies to creativity.

Your negathought could be restated in several ways. One way might be, *I have never learned a process for creative problem solving*. There are many tools available to help people become more creative. There are books on creativity, seminars, and computer software for generating ideas. Some of us are just creative by nature. Even this natural creativity can be enhanced by processes and tools designed to spawn ideas. For the many of us who may not be naturally creative, these tools can provide a significant boost to us as we attempt to think in new and innovative ways. If your problem, as you restate it, is that you have never learned techniques for increasing your own personal creativity, then this restatement opens the door for you to learn techniques and acquire the necessary tools to increase your creativity and solve problems more creatively.

In work situations, sometimes our negathoughts are very specific. Rather than the general, *I'm not creative*, it may take the form of, *I'm not creative enough to come up with a new ad campaign*. A rephrasing of this negathought might be, *I don't have the background to be able to design this ad campaign*. This would be a realistic assessment—that you have not developed the background to be able to do a given task. You now have a choice to learn how to develop an ad campaign by studying under someone else, acquiring a mentor, attending a class or workshop, or just reading about how ad campaigns work. That is very different from telling yourself that you are not creative.

Here is one final example. Let's say your negathought is, *Nobody understands me*. Many of us feel that others don't understand us. What we often fail to acknowledge is that it's our own behaviors or activities that often can leave others puzzled or wondering what's going on with us. If you reflect on why people don't understand you, you might discover that you tend to keep things to yourself and don't communicate your thoughts or feelings readily to others. If this were the case, your thought that *nobody understands me* might be rephrased to say, *I don't always communicate my feelings in a way that helps people understand my issues*.

Again, what you have done for yourself in the second statement is to empower yourself by acknowledging that you do not always communicate effectively. You now have options available to improve your communications. You could take a course in communications, or you could merely make a conscientious effort to be more communicative with others and solicit their feedback to determine if they feel you are communicating more effectively with them. This is very different from a broad-based statement like, *Nobody understands me*, something you can do nothing about. If nobody understands you, there's not much point in communicating anything.

To develop your takeover mentality, try to establish your own internal trigger every time you find yourself in a negathought. Trigger yourself into challenging the negathought and asking yourself, *How can I restate this negathought so that I have some choice or power in the situation?* The key is to practice rethinking your negathoughts, and to make it a habit.

Following is an exercise that involves taking a look at some of your negathoughts, this time rewriting them in such a way as to allow yourself choice. On the worksheet that follows, write down some of the negathoughts you identified earlier (page 109), or perhaps others that have come to mind. Once you have identified these negathoughts, sit back for a moment and reflect on each. Then rewrite those thoughts. Try to make a realistic assessment of the situation, and write your thoughts in a way that shows that you could potentially change things, should you decide to do so.

If you're having trouble rewriting your negathoughts, the following tips and techniques might prove helpful:

- Question your absolutes. Most negathoughts suggest that you are absolutely the worst at something or that there is one and only one way of interpreting events. Absolute words such as *always* and *never* are red flags. When you see these statements, ask yourself if you've exaggerated—if you've taken a few bad experiences and blown them up into an absolute statement. What might be a more realistic way of expressing the cause of your bad experiences?
- Identify the feeling beneath the negathought. We sometimes think in negative terms because of how an experience made us feel. We think we're the biggest dummy in the universe because we made a mistake that caused

the team to miss its deadline. The feeling causes us to "globalize" an isolated incident. Look at your nega-thought and determine how you felt when the event or experience that spawned the thought took place. Did you feel angry or sad? Were you ashamed or depressed? How intense was the feeling; on a scale of 1 to 10 (with 1 being the lowest intensity), how would you rank the feeling? Odds are, you experienced an intense feeling, and this created an illogical negathought. Recognizing this fact will help you get past this way of thinking.

- Reflect on what type of education, experience, or expertise might solve the problem raised by the nega-thought. In other words, what can you do that would help you deal better with the issue your negathought raises? For instance, if you think, *I'm the world's worst speaker*, are there any experiences or courses that might change that thought? Focus on the gap in your work background that causes you to think negatively in this situation. In the vast majority of cases, people can fill that gap through training or simply gaining experience in a given area.

- Separate the reality of what you do from the fantasy of who you think you are. The former is a mindset that will give you choices; the latter is a thought process that will box you into a corner of your mind. In earlier examples, people realized that their nega-thoughts emanated from specific things they did, like not communicating clearly or possibly being in positions that didn't encourage creative problem-solving. Look for the specific behaviors that cause problems in your job or in your career. These specific actions will give rise to all sorts of options for correction. Don't settle for the melodramatic negathought and leave yourself without options.

Rewriting Your Negathoughts to Allow Choice	
Original Negathought	**Rewritten Negathought to Allow Choice**

Jennifer was a leadership training consultant who had built a good business. With an MBA from a state college and 10 years experience doing leadership training at a mid-sized farm products company, she had starting her consulting firm five years ago and built it to the point that she had seven employees, a core of good clients, and a strong reputation in a few key industries. Jennifer, however, was frustrated. After steady growth for the first three years, her business leveled off. Despite her best efforts, she couldn't get any leadership training assignments from Fortune 100 companies, an area Jennifer felt was crucial for her firm's growth.

Let's take a look at the type of negathoughts dominating Jennifer's mind and how she could rewrite these. Here are Jennifer's rewritten negathoughts:

Rewriting Your Negathoughts to Allow Choice

Original Negathought	Rewritten Negathought to Allow Choice
Big corporations have no interest in working with me.	*I don't have the contacts in big corporations to enable me to easily gain a foothold in that market.*
I'm not strategic enough to suit large corporate executives.	*My MBA program didn't emphasize strategy, which shows when I talk with company executives who are strategic thinkers.*
People see me as a yokel who can only train farm company executives and no one else.	*I haven't shown executives how the programs our company has provided to farm executives are every bit as effective in other industries.*

Jennifer's restated negathoughts provided her with all sorts of alternatives. For instance, when she established that one roadblock to growth was her lack of contacts in large companies, she generated a number of options:

- Hire someone who has worked in a Fortune 100 company.
- Join a trade association whose members include top corporate executives.
- Bring in a partner who has contacts she is missing.

Jennifer eventually chose the last option and within the year, her business grew by 25 percent.

Negathoughts are often driven by external events

To see how powerful this illusion of being powerless is, consider what has happened to the stock market in the last two years. Since it began dropping, many people have seen a large portion of their 401(k)s or other investments dissipate. Some people have seen 50 percent or more of their investment portfolio vanish. In the face of this loss, they say to themselves, "I've lost so much due to the market collapse I can't ever retire, unless somehow the market does a miraculous rebound."

Stockbrokers themselves often fall prey to the successes and downturns of the stock market. Paul, a senior manager of a large brokerage firm, says that whenever the stock market turns down, you can see the slump among the brokers themselves. Many of them let their spirits rise and fall based on the fortunes or the downswings of the market. "Think about how ridiculous it is," he says, "when a broker lets something as crazy and irrational as daily market swings affect his mood. I know guys who are working on their second and third heart attacks, and I tell you it's because they have no sense of personal grounding—they have given control over their personal lives to the market."

Think about the absurdity of giving up control over your own life to something as uncontrollable as the market. Let's say that you have determined that you will need 70 percent of your current annual income during retirement. The drop in stock value could definitely impact your ability to derive this type of retirement income. As long as you stick steadfastly to your current definition of what retirement will look like, you'll remain hemmed in. If you apply takeover thinking and rewrite the negathought, you might say something like, *The market has dealt me a terrible setback. I am now going to have to explore various options for retirement.* This restatement frees you up to consider many different options for your retirement years.

To keep your options open, you need to put external events in perspective and refuse to let them throw you into a fatalistic victim mode. To that end, here's a multiple choice quiz that will help you simulate how you might think and what you might do under certain circumstances.

The external events quiz

1. Your company's stock plummets, and the company is rumored to be on the brink of declaring bankruptcy due to accounting fraud. You like the company and your particular job—you've described it in the past as a dream job—but the rumors are flying in the media and in the office. Would you:

   A. Automatically assume that you're soon going to be out of a job and tell yourself you have the worst luck in the world.

   B. Moan and groan to everyone in the office about the rumors and how management stinks.

   C. Reassure yourself that you might still have a job if the company survives because of your particular skills.

D. Tell yourself that if the worst happens you'll still be in a marketable job position because of all you've learned working for this organization.

2. Your boss and mentor leaves the organization to take another job. Would you:

A. Feel like you failed to be politically astute once again.

B. Think about how there's no way you could join your boss at the new company because it's located in another state.

C. Tell yourself that you have formed good relationships with other people in the company and that there still may be a place for you.

D. Look at the situation as an opportunity for advancement or at least a chance to learn from someone new.

3. You own your own company, and you form a partnership with another company, but it doesn't work out. Would you:

A. Swear never to form any partnerships or other types of alliances with anyone else ever again.

B. Think that partnerships might work for others but remain doubtful that you can make one work.

C. Tell yourself that you are a good partner but that you have to be more careful about deciding with whom you will partner.

D. Be open to other partnerships and assume you'll be a better partner in the future based on this failure— now you know what *not* to do.

4. You and two other people—one a current employee and another from outside the organization—are the final candidates for a plum position in your company. The outsider is chosen for the position. Would you:

A.   Be convinced that you lack the knowledge and skills to be selected for a top job.

B.   Blame internal politics for your situation, and tell yourself that the company wanted an outsider all along.

C.   Think that you were probably qualified for the job but that you should be more realistic about the positions you apply for.

D.   Recognize that the company probably made the right selection and that even being considered for the position was a good sign, signifying that they thought you had the skills necessary for a key job.

5.   You've been out of work for a month and have failed to land a single interview. Would you:

A.   Tell yourself that you're unemployable.

B.   Blame the economy or a suspected poor reference from your former employer for your plight.

C.   Decide that you are marketable but need more time and effort before you should judge yourself.

D.   Think that there must be more productive ways to go about getting interviews and that your challenge is to discover those avenues.

As you assess your answers, note that A and B answers represent victim mindsets, whereas C and D answers represent takeover mindsets.

There's always a choice

The concept of *choice* is critical to takeover thinking, because it helps each of us realize that there exist a variety of routes to success and personal fulfillment. True takeover thinkers have the capacity to adapt, change direction, and find opportunity in the most unlikely of circumstances. Their success is directly attributable to their willingness to see more than one path when facing crossroads in their work, career, or personal lives.

As you move closer to your takeover, concentrate on the type of thinking that offers you choices. You can do this by believing in and appreciating yourself rather than letting outside problems and obstacles shape how you view yourself. As Virgil stated, "They can because they think they can." This isn't mindless positivism but a mindful sense that there are many possible ways for you to achieve your goals. Takeover thinking is a belief in yourself—a belief that you can either accomplish what you initially set out to accomplish or that you can vary your route and redefine your life as you travel along your particular journey—and a commitment to always move in a positive direction.

When entire groups employ takeover thinking

Takeover thinking is happening all around us. If we just choose to look for it, we can find examples to inspire our own search for the positive in what sometimes appears to be a sea of helplessness and negativity. Sometimes we can witness dramatic examples, such as when a group of people, or even an entire community, chooses to leave the negathinking behind and employ takeover thinking.

The attack on the World Trade Center on September 11, 2001 was a supreme act of victim thinking. The terrorists who attacked the twin towers and the Pentagon were engaged in the most hideous type of win-lose mindset one can imagine.

This appalling example of victim thinking and an unproductive mindset led to many examples of people making choices to invest in others, to help those who were suffering, and to show that this world is made up of some very good people. For instance, shortly after the terrorist attack, the USS Winston Churchill, a United States destroyer, was placed on patrol off the coast of Europe. They had been at liberty, moored in Plymouth, England, when they were given instructions to begin patrolling a grid at sea. While in dock, the American sailors had spent time with sailors from the German destroyer, FGS Lutjens, which had also been moored in Plymouth. The sailors from the two countries had spent a day together playing sports and enjoying a cookout. Now the USS Winston Churchill was on a tedious mission, patrolling a grid in the ocean.

During the patrol, the Winston Churchill received a call from the Lutjens. The captain of the Lutjens was requesting permission to pass the Winston Churchill on the port side so that they could say good-bye to the American sailors. Permission was granted, and the captain of the USS Winston Churchill requested the crew of the American destroyer to come on deck to see the German sailors.

As the German ship approached, the crew could see that the FGS Lutjens was flying the American flag at half mast. Further, all the German sailors were lined up along the rail in their dress blues. A sign was displayed along the side of their ship. It said, "We stand by you." The German sailors saluted the Americans, and the Americans saluted back with tears in their eyes at this display of compassion and support. At this moment, an entire crew decided to engage in takeover thinking, deciding to cross cultural divides and show their support for their American comrades.

Scenario

The town of Gander, Newfoundland and its surrounding communities in the eastern part of Canada was the site of another mammoth display of takeover thinking on September 11 and the few days following.

Delta Airlines Flight 15 was over the Atlantic on a flight to Atlanta, Georgia, when a message was received from Delta headquarters. The message said something to the effect that all airways over the continental United States were closed, and Delta Flight 15 was to land at the nearest airport as soon as possible.

The captain of the plane determined that the closest airport was in Gander, Newfoundland, so he radioed Gander and was immediately given permission to land by the Canadian air traffic controller. They landed 40 minutes later, finding a number of airplanes from different countries already on the ground. By this time, the crew had some minimal information regarding the terrorist attacks on the United States, so they informed the passengers of what they knew. The atmosphere among the passengers transformed quickly from one of frustration and anger at having to abort their flight to Atlanta to shock and concern over what was happening in the U.S.

The flight landed around 12:30 in the afternoon, Gander time. The crew and passengers were required to remain on their airplane until the airport could figure out a way to disembark all of the planes that were landing. They finally left the plane at 10:30 the next morning. By now there were 53 planes from various nations at the Gander airport. A convoy of school buses transported the passengers from the portable stairway to the terminal. The crew was separated from the passengers and remained separated during the next few days in Gander. While the crew, after passing immigration, was transferred to a small hotel in Gander, they had no idea what had happened to the passengers.

They spent the next three days in Gander. Because so many planes were now stranded in Gander, there was no way that one community could absorb all of the passengers. Gander has a population of approximately 10,000, and there were over 10,000 passengers to be housed. Each of the neighboring towns joined together with Gander to provide hospitality to all of the new visitors. For about 75 kilometers around Gander, towns closed schools and converted them to housing areas. They used lodges, halls, and any facilities capable of being converted to sleeping quarters. Families made rooms available in their homes for the stranded passengers.

The passengers from Delta Flight 15 ended up in Lewisporte, Newfoundland, about 45 kilometers from Gander. They stayed in the high school, where the students pitched in and adopted passengers. The families were housed together. Older passengers were invited to stay with residents of Lewisporte. During each of these days, the passengers from Flight 15 were offered side trips to the forest or boating trips. Bakeries were baking fresh bread daily for the guests. Residents were bringing their home cooking to the school in Lewisporte to feed the stranded passengers. Passengers were also given the option to eat out at the local restaurants. They were given tokens to use at the laundromat, so that their clothes would remain fresh. They were provided telephone facilities to contact their loved ones back in the states.

On the morning of September 14, word was received that the air space above the U.S. was once again open to commercial traffic. School buses transported the passengers back to the plane from Lewisporte. At 12:30 p.m., Flight 15 left Gander to continue its journey to Atlanta. A flight attendant remarked that as the passengers boarded the plane, they were behaving as if they had been on a cruise. They knew each other by first names, and all were talking about the wonderful time they had in Lewisporte. The passengers exchanged names, phone numbers, and addresses and vowed to keep in touch.

Given the disaster that befell the U.S. and the discomfort and discombobulation that impacted both Gander residents and the passengers, adopting a victim mentality would have been a natural reaction. It's easy to imagine the people of Gander resenting the "intruders" and blaming them for disrupting their lives. Similarly, it's not difficult to picture passengers raging at the airlines and stewing for three days because they were "stuck in the middle of nowhere."

Instead, the vast majority of people assumed a takeover mindset. With the model of hospitality being demonstrated by the people of Gander, Newfoundland, thousands of passengers learned that though certain external events were outside of their control, they were in charge of what the next few days in Gander would be like for them. As a result, they discovered numerous choices. Passengers explored various options for spending their time in Gander, from forming new relationships to sampling the local cuisine to learning about the local culture; they were opening themselves to different possibilities.

The people in Gander and surrounding communities showed that, although their towns were small, they could provide many choices for the stranded passengers, and they became quite creative in not only providing physical and emotional support, but also providing entertainment for the stranded passengers. They saw the situation as an opportunity to assist people in need as well as to get to know people they might never know under other circumstances.

The attack on the World Trade Center was a situation that started with disaster—an incredible victim-oriented act, where terrorists, who somehow saw themselves as victims of the United States, chose to turn into persecutors and kill thousands of innocent people. This terrible display of the win-lose mindset led to an outpouring of humanity. The crew of a German destroyer and the residents of small Canadian towns turned despair into hope and optimism through their own personal heroism—both examples of great takeover thinking.

Chapter 9

How to Convert Victim Thinking Into Takeover Thinking

" " *You keep telling me I can't, so just can it, cuz' I think I can."*

You're now ready to get over the hump, to make good on your takeover offer. If you've been completing the exercises from the previous chapters, you'll find that you're well-prepared to convert yourself or someone you care about from victim to takeover thinking. You've already started to shift your view of reality in a more productive direction, and the ideas and tools you'll find here will help you complete this shift.

You'll find 12 steps that will enable you to make this conversion, and some of them will be familiar. Earlier, I've asked you to do parts of some of these steps. For instance, one of the steps involves rewriting negathoughts. Though you can use the rewriting exercise from Chapter 8, you'll see that the approach here is more integrated and formal—you're going to be rewriting your negathoughts as part of the larger takeover process. You'll learn how to use these rewritten negathoughts to launch your takeover.

As you go through these steps, keep in mind the lesson from the last chapter: Success is a choice. Even if you're in the doldrums because of a bad job or no job, you have the ability to choose your thoughts. Choice involves taking stock of things, and realizing that you are probably better off than what you might have otherwise thought. Cynthia Lewis, an inspirational writer, said, "Even if you have been fishing for three hours and haven't gotten anything except poison ivy and sunburn, you are still better off than the worm."

You can choose to be a takeover thinker and fill your head with productive thoughts designed to achieve objectives, or you can choose negathoughts that work against accomplishment.

Begin the process with step one.

1. Identify a specific negathought and determine whether it is chronic.

You can be a takeover thinker and have negative thoughts. If your boss treats you unfairly and asks you to work on the weekend even when he promised he wouldn't, you're naturally going to think, *That was really low—my weekend is ruined*. While it's great if you can find a positive aspect to this type of scenario, sometimes it's pretty difficult. You're disappointed or angry, and your thinking will reflect these feelings. When this thinking becomes chronic, however, you start lapsing into the victim mode.

Chronic negathoughts represent an ingrained pattern. They've implanted themselves into our brains, waiting to surface when certain situations arise. We slip into this thinking as easily and as unconsciously as an old sweater. Negathoughts do their damage to our work and our careers when they become a habit.

When I was in my 20s, I worked for a bank. The branch I managed was within 10 minutes of my house. I received an offer to move into Personnel, operating in downtown Detroit. I jumped at the chance, and started the new position. It was January, and in my first two days, two major snowstorms caused my drive to take about an hour and a half each way. I was beside myself. I remember saying, "I can't take this drive. It will kill me." I found myself becoming angrier and angrier about the slow moving traffic. After the second day, I realized I either had to change jobs or change my view of things. As I thought about it that second day, I realized that I am normally a very impatient person, and I often react negatively to traffic jams.

I realized my negathought was chronic—I always react negatively when my patience is tested, and especially when it's tested because of traffic jams. Recognizing this chronic condition helped me target a vulnerable area I needed to work on. We can become overwhelmed when we think about all the different types of negathoughts we might have every day. The key to beginning a personal takeover is to start by focusing on the negathoughts that are repeated most often and have the greatest potential impact on our current sense of well-being and on our future.

To help you identify your chronic negathoughts, create a negathought journal. For a period of time—a few weeks to a few months—jot down negathoughts that cross your mind. You can use the negathought chart in Chapter 6 (page 109) as a way to keep alert for certain negathoughts, but the key is to see which ones appear regularly. A negathought is chronic when you see the same negative sentiment recurring in different situations. For instance, you write, "This is never going to work out," when you get a new boss, when you are assigned a new project, or when your company merges with another organization.

Remember, too, that you can express the same basic negathought in different ways; your words may vary, but the sentiment remains the same. One journal entry might read, "I can never do anything right." Another one might be, "I always mess up these assignments." A third might be written as, "I'm just no good at this." These are all variations on the same theme.

The odds are that you have a relatively small number of chronic negathoughts. Keep a list of these chronics—both at work and at home—so that you become highly aware of their existence.

2. Trace a chronic negathought to its source.

Is it a thought you've had as long as you can remember? Is it a thought that is based on comments one of your teachers made in school? Can you trace its origins to a work situation? It helps to identify when the thought began, so you can have some understanding of its origins and why it sticks with you. Pinning down the negathought's beginning will loosen its hold. When you see that a negathought is rooted in events long past— and that it has little relevance to your life today—you will find it easier to let it go.

In searching for the thought's origins, look for a traumatic incident or emotionally troubling situation. An obvious one at work is getting fired or reprimanded in a particularly humiliating way. In school, it's receiving a poor grade or being embarrassed in front of the class. Look for the event that sticks out in your memory—one that you can't remember without a shudder.

Once you find this event or situation, accept that it no longer has the power to control you, and that no matter how awful or upsetting it was then, it has no relevance to who you are and what you do today. If you think it will help, make this a verbal renunciation. To yourself or to a trusted friend or advisor, affirm that you are no longer willing to let a stale negathought dominate your present mindset.

Searching for a negathought's origins sometimes can take you pretty far back into the past. When I first started thinking about why I became upset in traffic congestion, I couldn't find its source in recent history. But, as I thought about it more, I discovered something very interesting. My family was pretty poor, so it was not often that I had opportunities to go somewhere special. Whenever we did, I remember worrying that we would be late, or not make it at all. I would get so worked up, at times, that I actually became sick and was unable to attend the event.

While this discovery has not and will not eliminate my immediate negative reaction to heavy traffic situations, it has made me more aware of why I react the way I do and gives me a context that helps me both manage this chronic nega-thought and reduce my sense of frustration while driving in heavy congestion.

3. Determine basic assumptions that might be wrong.

You can't launch a personal takeover unless you challenge your assumptions. Place yourself in the following scenario: You go to a cocktail party because your boss has asked you to do so. Upon entering, you walk over to the refreshment table, grab a few hors d'oeuvres, and then go stand in a corner by yourself. You observe the crowd, realizing how uncomfortable you feel in this type of social situation. The thought comes to mind: *These people don't want to be talking to me. They don't even know me. I have nothing to offer them.* This is a chronic negathought, going back to the time when your father was transferred, and you had to attend a new school where you were initially convinced that all the kids hated you and thought you were a dork.

Now, think about your assumption that these people don't want to talk to you. Might this assumption be wrong? Of course it might. You might find that some of them are as terrified of speaking to others as you are. They might be thinking precisely the same thing you are thinking.

When I was reviewing my traffic-based negathoughts, here are some of the false assumptions I made:

- Everyone else will be to work on time.
- It's like this every time it snows.

There was nothing productive about these assumptions. Instead, they only succeeded in ratcheting up my anxiety level. Therefore, question your assumptions and search for flaws in your reasoning using the following techniques:

- Ask a trusted coworker or friend about your assumption; does he feel it's valid?
- Test your assumption with scientific rigor. Let's say your chronic negathought is that no one wants to talk to you at social functions. Your assumption underlying this negathought is that people don't want to talk to you because you have nothing interesting to say. Therefore, the next time you're talking to a friend or coworker with whom you feel comfortable, see how they react to you. Do they seem to be enjoying the conversation? Are they responding with enthusiasm and emotion? Observe if they're nodding off or if their eyes are glazing over when you're talking. If they do seem to be nodding off, grab them by the collar, pull them close to you, nose to nose, and shout, "What kind of a friend are you? Don't you see I'm talking to you?" Then tell them you're kidding and try to figure out why they were nodding off. By subjecting your hypothesis to this experiment, you can determine if your assumptions are valid.
- Analyze your assumptions using logic. Too often, we form our assumptions based on poor or scanty evidence. We can often discover the flaws when we look at assumptions with rigorous logic. Let's say your chronic negathought is that you're never going to get promoted,

and this is based on your assumption that you need an MBA to be promoted. Logically, then, everyone in your organization who has been promoted will have an MBA. Is this true?

It's amazingly easy to form false assumptions that fuel our chronic negathoughts, but it's also possible to identify these false assumptions by doing a little testing and analysis.

4. Consider the consequences of maintaining this thinking.

By thinking about consequences, we acknowledge to ourselves that these negathoughts do have consequences for us. In the case of the cocktail party, the consequences are that you will likely not talk to anybody. Or if you do end up speaking with somebody, you might be so concerned about them not wanting to be talking with you that you keep the conversation very trivial and light. As a result, they may lose interest very rapidly and walk away.

Make a list of consequences that demonstrate the impact of your chronic negathoughts. Be very specific when creating the list. What exactly happens when you think that only brown-nosers get ahead in your organization? How does this affect your relations with peers and bosses? Do you lack the energy and initiative to work extra hard or make commitments to get jobs done to the best of your ability?

Typically, the consequences of chronic negathoughts are self-fulfilling prophecies. We think bad things happen to us, and bad things do happen to us. The consequences, however, are a result of our thinking rather than the curse we think we're under. Seeing how we create our own negative consequences through our thinking is a real incentive to adopt a takeover mentality.

5. Generate options.

When you've gone through the earlier steps of identifying chronic negathoughts and recognizing their consequences, you'll find that you gain a certain amount of freedom to choose. The more conscious you are of how your negathoughts lock you into one particular pattern of behavior, the better able you'll be to free yourself from that pattern.

As I emphasized in the previous chapter, success is a choice, and when you establish your takeover, you have many choices. At this point, you want to concentrate on generating options, especially when you encounter problems or obstacles. These options will help you approach a difficult situation differently. With your negathoughts out of the way—or at least being consciously managed—you'll find it easier to accept that you have options, and this will grant you the freedom to change.

Let's return to our cocktail party example. One option is for you to go to the party and stand in the corner. Before, when your boss asked you to go, this seemed like your only option. Now, though, you've looked at the consequences of your chronic negathoughts and realized that your boss won't be particularly pleased that you failed to network, because that was why he wanted you to go in the first place. In fact, he'll probably talk to you once again about how, if you have any aspirations of moving up in the organization, you have to start learning how to form and manage new relationships. You also realize the assumptions upon which your negathought is based may be incorrect.

Therefore, you might consider other alternatives. One alternative, of course, is simply not to attend the party. Obviously, this will not have positive consequences, but you may decide you belong in another job or profession where this type of social activity isn't required. Another option is attending the party and forcing yourself to talk to everyone you encounter. This thought might feel overwhelming and discourage you from trying to interact. But you have yet another option, that of making a small but concerted effort to talk to three people at the party. This is a modest goal, and you might even become excited about this option because suddenly, it seems very doable.

In the case of my drive downtown, an option would have been to quit the new job and go back to the branch. Another option would have been moving closer to the new location. A third option would have been to not do anything and have a heart attack in three years. The option I finally chose was to leave a half hour earlier most mornings and get extra work done, and to give myself a mental message when I began the drive each day that I would be totally calm no matter what happened. I would accomplish so much more by being early most days that no one would be upset if I were occasionally late due to weather.

Here's a technique you might find useful to generate options for yourself. Focus on the only choice that seemed available to you in a given situation because of your negathought. Maybe when faced with a company that seemed to have lost its way and with little prospect for advancement, you figured your only option was to hang in there and hope things would get better. Open up your thinking by focusing on "option extremes." In this case, one extreme option might be resigning and immediately looking for another job. At the other extreme, it might be sitting down with your boss and volunteering to devote yourself to coming up with a way to help the organization get back on its feet.

The extremes you come up with don't have to be realistic; they're designed simply to show you that you have a wide range of potential options. Once you create your extremes, see how many options for action you can create that reside in between.

6. Rewrite your negathought to acknowledge that you have the ability to change.

With your various options in mind, rewrite your chronic negathought so that you leave open the possibility of doing things differently. In our cocktail party example, instead of the thought that nobody wants to speak to you, you might reword the negathought as follows: *I often don't prepare interesting things to say at cocktail parties or plan out how I will approach various people.* Now you have given yourself a way to approach this situation differently.

In rewriting your negathought, focus on words that allow your options room to breathe. Too often, we think in such narrow terms that it appears as if our circumstances won't allow us to change. In reality, we're the ones who are hampering our ability to do things differently.

For instance, Ben maintained for years that he couldn't work on teams. He told himself that he was an individualist and that teamwork stifled his creativity and initiative. It took him a while, but Ben finally was able to admit to himself, *My trouble with teams is that I've resisted acquiring the team-building and communication skills that are important to being effective in team settings.* With this acknowledgment, Ben was able to change and adapt his style to the team structures that had become prevalent in his organization.

7. Identify messages you can give yourself that would be productive in a given circumstance.

By productive, I mean confident, relaxed, and able to achieve the goals that are important to you. Think about what you might tell yourself that would enable you to feel in control and help you achieve what you want to achieve. For the cocktail party, you might say, *Some of them may not want to talk to me, but I am going to show them how important it is that they had a chance to meet me.* In the case of the commute to work, I told myself, *This is a small price to pay for a wonderful opportunity, and I can remain calm in traffic because there is nothing so important that it is worth jeopardizing my health.*

Concentrate not on what a situation is preventing you from accomplishing, but on what you can accomplish despite the limitations of the situation. Remember, there may well be things happening in your work environment that are negative—bad bosses, political coworkers, and economic downturns—but that doesn't mean you have to think in negative terms.

To find the productive messages inside of you, do the following:

- Think about how a given individual or a group would benefit if they knew what you know.
- Examine a negative event from an opportunistic perspective; search for a way you can turn what seems like a bad thing into a good one; rotate a situation in your mind like it's one of those "hidden picture" drawings, so that you're viewing it from a perspective that reveals a positive aspect.
- Concentrate on how your involvement with a situation might change things; consider what you're particularly well-qualified to contribute that might change opinions, surprise, delight, and impress.

8. Create a worst-case scenario for changing your thoughts in this circumstance.

This step is very important in that it helps us to see that the consequences of changing our thoughts are typically nowhere near as catastrophic as we originally anticipated. We often fall short of personal takeovers because of unstated or unacknowledged consequences. In my work with managers, I see it all the time. People are afraid to speak in public, afraid to go out on sales calls, afraid to propose an exciting but risky plan. These fears often freeze us, because we have unstated consequences that in many cases are unrealistic and never come about. With most activities, for instance, it would be highly unlikely for the consequence to be that we would die as a result of the activity, or in a work situation, that we would figuratively die by being terminated. By identifying the worst possible consequence, we see that the actual consequences are probably far less terrible than we might have thought.

For instance, what is the worst possible consequence of going up and talking to people at the cocktail party? Let's watch another person, Bill, who has been as fearful as you, but has worked to build up the courage to talk with others at the party.

Bill sees two fellows over in the corner talking. They look safe enough, one dressed in a linen sport coat and the other in black. He walks over...

Scenario

"Hello, gentlemen."

The two other men abruptly halt their conversation. One looks at Bill suspiciously. "You the messenger?"

"What messenger?" inquires Bill nervously.

"The one big Al was sending with the goods. Hey, what's this, a setup? Rico, we got a man here who's got to be taken out. Okay, buddy, walk slowly in front of us. We're going to leave the property."

Well, let's leave Bill for now. He's about to have an interesting experience he just wouldn't have had if he hadn't gotten the nerve up to talk to those two interesting men.

What are the worst possible consequences of approaching someone at a cocktail party? As you read the dialogue between Bill and the two gentlemen, you probably thought something like *How ridiculous! This would never happen. Why did he throw this silly example in here?* The reason I threw this example in is precisely to show how silly it is. Yet, when people don't engage in this exercise of identifying the worst possible consequence, my experience is that they have an unstated, subconscious consequence that is something akin to *I'll die if I have do that.* So we construct a huge barrier in our subconscious minds that mimics Bill's scenario and prevents us from a personal takeover.

To bring the worst possible consequences out into the open, do the following:

A.   List a rewritten negathought and all the negative repercussions if you were to think this way. Don't exaggerate or list ridiculous things. Instead, consider what your fears would be if you thought in this manner. How might your boss react? Your peers? Your direct reports? Your customers? What are the worst reactions these people might have?

B.   Divide the list into Unacceptable and Acceptable Consequences.

C.   Of the Unacceptable Consequences, how likely are they to happen? List the odds of each one of them happening.

D.   Of the Unacceptable Consequences with high odds of taking place, is there a tradeoff that would move an Unacceptable Consequence into the Acceptable category (for instance, if you gained a promotion only after undertaking a task you have long been avoiding, would it be worth it?).

Most people find that this exercise greatly diminishes the power of worst-case scenario consequences. These consequences are magnified when they float around in our heads as vague fears. When we pin them to the board and analyze them, however, they become much less scary and often cease to be an obstacle to a personal takeover.

9. Focus on the best-case scenario.

Flip back to the previous step and look at how changing your thinking might make good things happen for you in your work or business. In other words, give yourself an incentive to be a takeover thinker. What might happen if you started telling yourself that your unique blend of skills makes you eminently marketable? Some of the good things that might happen include obtaining a significant raise, finding a new job with much more reward and recognition, and using this newfound confidence to function more effectively and innovatively.

As in the previous step, you want to be realistic. It might be nice to think that you're going to be the next CEO of General Electric, but if you're a middle manager at a small company, that probably won't happen. At the same time, focus on how a shift in your thinking might solve a particularly vexing problem you're facing in your job or career, or how it might help you take advantage of an opportunity that previously seemed just out of reach. In fact, make a list of problems and opportunities you can target in this best-case scenario.

In the cocktail party situation we have been following, Bill saw two other gentlemen talking. He's already identified that the worst case would be if they're mob figures who don't want to talk with him. The best-case scenario might be that these two guys are CEOs of large companies and will be interested in doing business with his company. Or maybe they're talent scouts who will see his great potential as an actor (which might be a bit of a stretch, considering Bill's difficulty in even getting up the nerve to talk with them).

10. Picture yourself responding with takeover behaviors.

Visualize yourself in control of a situation where formerly you might have been controlled by other people or circumstances.

Picture yourself contemplating all the things you can do rather than all the things you can't achieve. Visualization will help you perceive yourself differently. By seeing yourself as possessing the authority and capability to accomplish specific objectives, you are setting up conditions for a more favorable outcome than in the past.

While there are many visualization techniques, I'd suggest simply closing your eyes in a quiet place and bringing to mind a familiar scenario. Imagine a familiar situation and how you thought and acted in the past. Recall your negative thoughts and specific actions, and how they produced an unsatisfactory result. Now wipe the slate clean and picture this familiar scenario again, only this time it's some point in the near future, and you're practicing takeover thinking. Walk yourself through this scenario and conclude with a positive ending.

Hold this scene in your head. It's a dress rehearsal for life as a takeover thinker.

11. Plan when you will turn your takeover thinking into action.

Anticipate situations where you will have the choice to respond differently than you have in the past. Don't just say, *I will respond differently at some point in time in the future.* Plan a time when you are going to make a clear change in how you respond to an individual, event, or situation using takeover techniques. Try to identify an opportunity or problem you want to deal with and create an action plan for confronting it in a new way.

It is one thing to say you are going to do something differently, yet it is another thing entirely to actually do it. We all know the old saying, "talk is cheap." Responding differently than you have in the past to certain situations is very difficult. You've been used to responding in a given way. If you don't consciously plan a different response it will be very difficult to implement it. In the heat of this familiar situation, you're likely to resort to your old negathinking and fall into old habits.

The plan I'm suggesting here doesn't have to be elaborate, but it does have to specify the time and/or situation when you're going to exercise takeover behavior.

12. Commit to respond this way in the next 10 opportunities.

If you want a particular way of thinking and acting to become a regular part of your psyche, you must repeat it. Just doing it one time will not work. In fact, you may stumble at first as you attempt to get the hang of being a takeover person. Think of any skill you have ever acquired. The first time you attempted to use it, you probably felt awkward. Things didn't turn out exactly as you may have envisioned. If you wish to change victim thinking into takeover thinking, expect to go through this same shaky learning phase.

Therefore, make a commitment to employ takeover thinking consistently. I've chosen the number 10, but the real key is the commitment to use personal takeover tactics repeatedly. This doesn't mean that you've failed if something happens and you find yourself falling back into old victim patterns. You do, however, need to practice takeover thinking in as many situations as possible until it becomes second nature and you truly have established your takeover.

☑ Takeover Rule #18: ☑

If you want to achieve
a personal takeover, it requires action.

An example of putting the 12 steps into practice

Jamie is a project manager. For a number of years, she's been stymied in her career. Her current employer, a multinational company, had seemed like a place that would give her many opportunities to advance. Jamie, however, wasn't able to take advantage of these opportunities, and she has been "stuck" at a project manager level for five years. The final straw was when she came up with an idea for a product promotion and had an opportunity to present it to the management team. Jamie presented her idea, but she left the meeting totally demoralized. Nobody listened to her. Instead, within moments after she began talking, others interrupted and carried the conversation to a different topic. They thanked her for her time and dismissed her—with no action taken. As she returned to her office, the dominant thought in her mind was, *Nobody listens to me. They just don't care what I think.* Jamie resolved to change and began using the lessons from this book to do so. Here is the 12-step worksheet she completed:

**1. Identify a specific negathought
and determine whether it is chronic.**

I often find that no one listens to me. I can cite at least 10 times in the past years when people acted like I was invisible when I made presentations or talked in team meetings.

2. Trace a chronic negathought to its source.

It has always appeared to me that my dad listened to my brother and seemed to take him seriously, but that he has never really listened to me—for as long as I can remember. My brother and sister seem to pay attention to one another, but always seem to tune me out when I begin talking. This has continued into my working life.

3. Determine basic assumptions that might be wrong.

That I am presenting my ideas ineffectively.

That others don't want to hear what I have to say.

That others don't respect me.

4. Consider the consequences of maintaining this thinking.

I'll continue to be ignored, and eventually my self-esteem will reach such a low point that I won't even care about doing a good job.

My resentment toward my boss and fellow workers will continue to build to the point that I won't even want to talk to them.

At some point, I'm going to have trouble contributing enough to even maintain my position as a project manager and won't have enough confidence to apply for jobs elsewhere.

5. Generate options.

Meet with my father, brother, and sister. Share my perception with them and ask for feedback on what can make me more effective.

Meet with a member of the management team to get feedback on my presentation.

Continue to use my victim thinking and get the same results.

Explore different approaches. In my next meeting I will not behave tentatively, but will instead be very assertive.

6. Rewrite your negathought, acknowledging that you have the ability to change.

I do not present my ideas as effectively or assertively as I could.

I have never learned a process for effective presentations.

7. Identify messages you can give yourself that would be productive in a given circumstance.

I am smart and my ideas are valuable, and my boss is always telling our group that he values great ideas above all else.

I can package ideas in a way that causes them to be heard, especially in some of our team meetings when everyone is competing for attention.

Others would like me to assertively state my thoughts; more than one person on our team has told me that I should contribute more in meetings because they know how much experience I have.

8. Create a worst-case scenario for changing your thoughts in this circumstance.

People will wonder why I'm acting so weird; they'll think it's strange that I'm suddenly being more assertive and taking up more time talking in meetings. They might resent my contributions and complain to my boss. Maybe even my boss will be confused about what's come over me.

9. Focus on the best-case scenario.

People pay attention to me; my performance review is great and there's no mention of how I'm unassertive. For the first time, I'm viewed as a key contributor because I command attention and respect in meetings. I'm promoted to a supervisory role.

10. Picture yourself responding with takeover behaviors.

I can see myself standing up and talking with great confidence in the next meeting. Instead of my usual soft voice and uncertain manner, I'm very clear and direct. I don't back off when people question me and I communicate my passion for and belief in the ideas I'm espousing. No one's attention

*wanders when I'm speaking and I make eye contact with people
rather than looking down at my shoes when I have the floor.*

**11. Plan when you will turn
your takeover thinking into action.**

The next meeting I attend.

**12. Commit to respond this way
in the next 10 opportunities.**

*There are six team meetings scheduled in the next three
months as well as one management meeting. In addition, I'm
part of a new virtual team that's been formed to coordinate
efforts in three different countries, and we're going to be meeting a lot in the next two months. In all these situations, I will
commit to practicing takeover thinking.*

You'll note that Jamie chose to fill out most of the steps on
the worksheet with brevity, which is fine. You may decide you
want to include more detail, which is great if it helps you. The
worksheet is designed to give you a way to chart your course
from victim to takeover thinker, but it's up to you to decide the
way in which you want to chart it. Jamie's choice worked for
her, since she eventually did receive her promotion and felt
much more in control of what was going on in her work life.

Creating your own chart

Before you fill out your own 12 steps, keep the following
points in mind. First, recognize that these 12 steps are insuffi-
cient without all the ideas and techniques that preceded them.
If I were to have presented you with these steps at the start of
the book, you probably would have struggled with them. You
might not have really believed it was possible for you to take
charge or have the control of a takeover thinker. You might
simply have bought into the process intellectually but not in
your heart. I hope that all the stories I've told you and the tools

I've shared made these 12 steps a natural evolution in the learning process. Plus, you still have a few lessons after these 12 steps to absorb that will make your takeover that much easier.

Second, a significant component of takeover thinking is optimism about your options. When you take these 12 steps in real life (as opposed to book life), you will demonstrate to yourself that you believe you have some control over your life and your future. Takeover thinking is neither fantasy nor denial. Some people think that, because it involves positive thinking, it is trite or Pollyannish, or that a person who remains optimistic when faced with adversity is naive. This couldn't be further from the truth. Takeover thinking is an approach that allows us to manage our future. It allows us to approach each day with the belief that we have options, and that we can make productive choices to move our lives forward. This is not a denial that life is tough. It is not living in a fantasy world. It is merely acknowledging that we have some ability to navigate within a world that can be challenging at times.

With these thoughts in mind, fill out the 12-step chart on page 180.

Completing the 12-step analysis I've provided in this chapter enables you to take a giant leap toward conquering fears or thoughts that have potentially held you back your entire life. As I have stated throughout this book, there is risk in shifting your view of a situation or a person. It is much easier to fall back on the views you've held throughout your life. It's understandable if you do.

I hope that you will just recognize the consequences of choosing to hold onto any negathought. Remember, you are where you are today because of the choices you've made, which have resulted from your basic mindset or view of the world. Depending on the extent to which negathoughts have dominated your mind, the choices you've made have probably limited your growth, success, and sense of well-being. The 12-step analysis is a powerful tool to help shift the course of your life toward more productive and satisfying results.

Converting Negathinking to Takeover Thinking

1. Identify a specific nega-thought and determine whether it is chronic.	
2. Trace a chronic negathought to its source.	
3. Determine basic assumptions that might be wrong.	
4. Consider the consequences of maintaining this thinking.	
5. Generate options.	
6. Rewrite your negathought, acknowledging that you have the ability to change.	
7. Identify messages you can give yourself that would be productive in a given circumstance.	
8. Create a worst-case scenario for changing your thoughts in this circumstance.	
9. Focus on the best-case scenario.	
10. Create an image of yourself responding productively.	
11. Plan when you will turn your takeover thinking into action.	
12. Commit to respond this way in the next 10 opportunities.	

Chapter 10

Testing the Takeover Waters

❝❝ *I'm surrounded by sharks,
so pass the fishing rod."*

NOW YOU'RE READY TO FLEX YOUR TAKEOVER MUSCLES.
Having left your victim thinking behind, you're capable of
great things. But how do you start? The transitional period,
moving from the victim to the takeover mindset, can be a bit
bewildering. Therefore, I'd like to offer you some techniques
here that will facilitate this transition. These techniques are
designed to help you become accustomed not only to being in
control of your work life, but seeing the impact takeover thinking has on people, projects, and your career. As you'll discover, the more you exercise your takeover power, the more
comfortable you'll become with it.

At first, expect some discomfort. Most of us have spent a
number of years having ceded control of our work life to others. To the extent you have engaged in victim thinking, you've
lived in a world where things seem to have been done to you.
You've battled with bosses, organizations, teams, partners, the
economy, the marketplace, and general circumstance. You may

not have done this consciously, but intent is irrelevant. For a long time, you've felt as if you were stuck in a job, with a company or in a career and there was little you could do to impact the stickiness of your situation. When people asked you (or you asked yourself) why you don't make a change, you offered up a series of excuses, defenses and rationalizations:

- The time isn't right.
- The economy is bad.
- The money's too good to leave.
- I don't have the training to do anything else.
- I'd feel like they won if I left now.
- I'd be crazy to try something else at this point in my career.

In reality, there was nothing preventing you from making a change except your own self-imposed and largely illusory limitations. Once you've given up this mindset, the sky's the limit. At first, however, it may not seem this way. During the transition, you may still be confused by lingering assumptions from those victim-thinking days. Perhaps the most common one—and the one that you're going to have to guard against now—is the assumption that your organization and your bosses are the enemy (if you have your own business, you may see your employees or your customers in this enemy role). You may have viewed the organization as wanting to get as much as possible from the employee while returning as little as possible.

☑ Takeover Rule #19: ☑

The only things preventing you from changing your life are your own self-imposed and largely illusory limitations.

Preparing yourself for residual victim thinking

As you launch your personal takeover, you need to free yourself from the residual effects of this victim mindset. To free yourself, you may benefit from what I've observed about organizations. Well-run companies want anything but victims. They want takeover thinkers and are prepared to reward them. They recognize that takeover mindsets add value to the organization; that when a crisis strikes or adversity hits, these are the people who can take positive action rather than lamenting all the problems the company faces. Takeover thinkers generate innovative alternatives and foster confidence in others that solutions can be found. As a result, astute executives are not interested in exploiting their people but in finding an equitable, win-win relationship with them. They know victim thinkers are a dime a dozen and takeover thinkers are key contributors. Therefore, don't let negathoughts about the organization deter you as you begin your personal takeover.

You should also be prepared for a few surprises in the early days of this takeover. First, you'll find that some individuals will have difficulty relating to you, especially those who have liked to play the "rescuer" or the "persecutor" with you. They may be bosses, direct reports, coworkers, suppliers, or customers, but in rescuer or persecutor modes, they needed you to think like a victim for them to fulfill their roles. A rescuer, for instance, needs someone to rescue—that's you. They need you to continually find reasons to rely on them. They need all of your excuses why things can't be accomplished. This is where they get a chance to jump in and help out, or it gives them the opportunity to empathize with you about your plight. A rescuer needs to be needed. So, they need a victim. If you are no longer a victim, they must seek out someone else.

The persecutors also have a stake in you staying exactly where you are. They'll be the real skeptics when you attempt to shift your mindset and your resulting behaviors. If you attempt to be collaborative in a situation where, in the past, you had a win-lose mindset, they'll be the first to look for the "real" reason you're doing it, reflexively suspecting you have ulterior motives.

In some cases, unfortunately, a persecutor will be your boss. I have observed how persecuting managers respond when their direct-reports with victim mindsets transition to takeover mindsets. It is not unusual for these bosses to be skeptical, refusing to believe the individual can change. It is typically only after repeated positive experiences that they are finally willing to concede that a change has occurred, and that this change is good for the individual and the organization.

Finally, be aware that even though you've done all the work necessary to embark on a successful personal takeover, your victim mentality will still tempt you. The victim position provides the illusion of power. Everything revolves around the victim. Bosses are concerned about your work and attempt to find ways to help you get it done. Rescuers console you and do some things for you to help you get by. Persecutors give you lots of attention, even if it's negative attention. Family members all look for their own ways to help you and spend much of their time focused on your particular needs. And other victims band with you against the organization and against those who would attempt to make things genuinely better. Remaining in the victim mode enables you to refrain from taking responsibility for your own life. The thinking goes, *As long as I can blame others for my condition, I don't have to do anything about it. I can avoid all the long hard work necessary in assuming responsibility for my future.*

If you find yourself in this situation, be aware that, though it may take a bit of time, bosses and others will eventually come around to your new way of thinking. Once your boss accepts that you are genuinely employing takeover thinking, he should be very receptive. Especially in a downsized, economically volatile environment, companies realize the value of a contributing employee. They will attempt to reward and retain those who most exemplify takeover traits. As you move through this transitional period, you'll start to see yourself presented with more opportunities for advancement and more rewarding projects than ever before. Instead of a world set against you, you're more likely to find a world that encourages you to keep in the game, if not promising a win every time.

As in a business takeover, you're not going to gain power overnight. When a company seeks to acquire another organization, they engage in a process that involves planning, strategy, negotiation, transitioning, and other activities. While a personal takeover isn't nearly as complicated as a business one, it is a process—a process that requires cognitive, psychological, and emotional shifts.

The following techniques will assist you in making these shifts:

Technique 1: When getting ready for work in the morning, create your mindset for the day.

You've established your takeover mindset. You're committed to thinking in this new way and excited about the possibilities. Revved up for the work week ahead, you can't wait to get started on your post-takeover life. And then you get up the next morning.

If you are like many people, your alarm clock goes off at an hour fit only for roosters and farmers. You're tucked in under the covers, all nice and cozy, when suddenly it is time to get out of that bed. You growl and yawn and think, *Oh no, I have to go to work.* You reach out to whack the snooze bar, but instead hit a half-filled glass of soda sitting on the nightstand and knock it to the floor. Eventually, you drag yourself out of bed—possibly after hitting the snooze button several more times and cursing the glass you knocked over—and begin the routine of preparing yourself to go to work. For some of us, this routine may last as little as 30 minutes. For others, it may take as long as two hours. You kick the soda glass on the floor several times before you finally pick it up and get a rag to wipe the floor. You take a shower, shave or put on your makeup, find some clothes to wear, and brush your hair. All the time spent getting ready this morning has been focused on your outward appearance.

You get into the car and drive to work, sometimes fighting traffic. Or you commute by bus or train, jammed into a small space with a lot of people, half of whom seem to be sneezing and wheezing and sending germs your way. By the time you arrive at work, you are in a miserable mood. You look great, but you're cranky. You walk in and see Melissa, who looks like she combed her hair with an eggbeater. You snap at her as you walk by, "Hey Melissa, I'm going to be retired before you get me that report you promised me." Before she swings at you, you rush to your desk, fall into your chair and grumble, "I need some cof-fee," as if you expect someone to actually go and get it for you. No one does, of course. People around you roll their eyes, try to ignore you, and all know to stay away until you've had your coffee and are less likely to snap their heads off.

It may be that your routine is slightly different. Maybe instead of arriving in the office as a grouch you enter as a frightened lamb, worried about who is going to yell at you or demand something from you. Perhaps you arrive in a state of complete and utter apathy and go through the day like an automaton.

Whatever your routine and demeanor, ask yourself, *Do I really want it to be this way? Or would I like an alternative?*

An option available to you is to create a morning mindset that transforms your routine. Most of us, however, never even consider doing this. How many of us, in the hour or two when we're getting ready to go to work, take even 15 seconds to look in the mirror and ask, "What kind of person am I going to be today?"

Think about the difference if you were to do that. Let's back it up even further. Think about the difference if, when the alarm clock went off, you were to say to yourself, "This is going to be a terrific day. I've got things to do that really mean something in my life, and I can't wait to get started on them."

Now you may think this is ridiculous, that you can't imagine looking forward to work like it was a chance to play your favorite golf course or travel to that beach of your dreams in Bora Bora. If this is how you feel, realize that you're letting your environment control your thinking rather than attempting to control your environment. People who complete successful personal takeovers can thrive in any environment or quickly find a new environment where they'll flourish.

If the statement above was too much for you, try something like, *I'm going to look for a positive alternative every time I face a problem today*. This is much simpler in that you only need concern yourself with responding positively when a potentially negative situation presents itself.

Therefore, suspend your disbelief and do as follows: When you get ready tomorrow morning, take a 15-second pause, look in the mirror, and say, *Today is going to be different, because I am going to_____*. Fill in the blank with words or phrases like *seek positive alternatives to my negathoughts*, *be open-minded about the organization*, *identify creative alternatives for every problem that arises*, or whatever else will make the day a better experience for you and those around you. You could identify a specific action you wish to take, like, *start a conversation with John, my boss's boss, because he seems like he really knows this business*, or, *contribute some ideas in our team meeting rather than sitting there like a bump* *on a log.* Don't worry about whether your statement is too trivial.

Do not, I repeat, do not complete the phrase by saying, *Today is going to be different, because I am going to tell Melissa what a creep I really think she is.* Trust me, if you do complete the sentence like that, then you need to reread the book—or get a frontal lobotomy.

Now, in the space provided, decide whatever you think will be a takeover thought for you to say to yourself tomorrow morning:

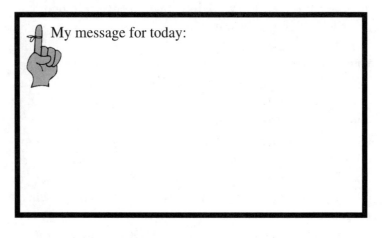

My message for today:

When you do this, you are advertising to yourself. We see the power of advertising in our daily lives. It influences our views and our desires. A classic example of the power of advertising was the launch of the Ford Mustang in 1964. An advertising campaign surrounded the launch of the mustang, using the theme "Mustang makes it happen!" Scenes in television commercials depicted an average fellow, stopped for a traffic light, who was suddenly surrounded by adoring women. There were reported instances, during the campaign, of men who drove their new Mustangs up to traffic lights and waited—waited for their Mustang to "make it happen!"

Apply the power of advertising to yourself. What is a message you would like to give yourself tomorrow morning? Write it down in the box, and, tomorrow morning, look yourself in the mirror and give yourself this message. Then at the end of the day, stop and give yourself a critique. Did you follow through on your morning plan? If not, try it again the next day and the days after that, until you do.

Technique 2: Do something today you would normally have been afraid to do.

Fear is paralyzing. It can prevent us from moving forward. Wayne Gretzky, considered one of the all-time best hockey players, once said, "You miss 100 percent of the shots you never take." Gretzky was right. If you don't take the risk, you are never going to have a chance to get what you want. A personal takeover requires you to face and overcome your fears, and this technique will move you in a courageous direction.

Not long ago, I was conducting a personal takeover seminar at a hospital. Afterwards, a nurse came up to me and said, "It happened to me in college. I went to a college dance. There was this guy I recognized from my English class. He was just standing there, talking to a few other guys. I wanted so much to go up and talk with him, and maybe even ask him to dance, but I couldn't. I just froze. I mean, it wasn't a girl's place to ask a guy to dance. And what if he turned me down? A few years later, I was working here at the hospital, and sure as shootin', he turns up as an intern. Well, he recognized me from college and we became friends. He's married now. One day, when we were talking about those days in college, he brought up the dance. And you know what he said? He said, 'I saw you over there with some girlfriends, and I wanted so much to come over and talk with you, and maybe ask you to dance, but I was afraid you'd say no.'"

Think about something you would normally be afraid to do and just do it. While it's fine to focus on your job or career, it doesn't have to be work-related. It might be something as simple as meeting somebody you have wanted to meet. It might be going somewhere alone. It might be placing a call to somebody to whom you haven't talked in a long time, even though you're afraid she might not want to talk to you. At work, it might be asking your boss for some additional responsibility. In your career, it might mean that you stop talking about how you'd love to be a teacher, and actually take an education class or two, to gauge your aptitude and interest.

When I talk about risk, I'm not advocating taking foolish risks. There are many things that scare us because they involve the chance of serious injury or involve very high stakes. You may dream of climbing Mount Everest, but this may not be the right time to risk your life. Similarly, quitting one's job and pursuing a dream career as a fishing guide involves significant financial risks, especially if you have a family to support. For our purpose of getting the "feel" of a personal takeover, focus on smaller fears or risks. There will be times when you must confront situations where the consequences could be great, such as putting your job on the line because you disagree with an action being taken within your organization. This type of risk should be taken after thoughtful consideration of the upsides and downsides.

Why is it so important to take a risk, and why is risk taking part of takeover thinking? First of all, you wouldn't be here if your parents hadn't taken the risk to have a child. Attending school involved the risk of failure. Learning to ride a bike involved the risk of injury. The more risk-averse we are, the harder it is to grow and achieve success. Very few companies are successful if they take a risk-averse posture. They must continually reinvent themselves, if they wish to survive. This involves risk. The same is true for us as individuals. All growth requires a risk.

If you're like most people, you won't have to search hard to find actions that scare you. Just about everyone misses opportunities on a daily basis because they're afraid to ask for something or state their opinion or simply act. Search your memory for an opportunity you missed because taking action made you anxious or nervous.

Here's an opportunity to identify a risk you want to take. In the following box, write down something you would like to say or do within the next two days that entails some degree of risk, but has the chance to yield some positive outcome for you:

My risk:	
I will:	When:

Technique 3: Force yourself to view a familiar problem from an unfamiliar perspective.

This is a difficult technique for many people because it challenges the picture of reality we have created for ourselves. Technique 3 requires that we be open and that we acknowledge that our idea or image may be wrong. This is very difficult for many of us to do. Yet, this is precisely what's needed to move you beyond your comfort zone, and to move you into a position where you can have a broader perspective.

If we never view an issue from a fresh perspective, we become convinced that there is only one perspective to view it from. As a result, we fail to see other possibilities and feel we don't have alternatives to our usual course of action. Viewing a familiar issue in a new way, however, demonstrates that our reality isn't sacrosanct; we don't have to be a prisoner of one way of seeing things. Shifting perspectives increases our sense of control. By doing so, we learn that we have the power to shift reality.

Some people have difficulty with this technique because it's scary to admit that what we always assumed was true is false. Yet it's worth facing our fear because it allows us to take over that part of ourselves that has always insisted on doing things one way.

One of the best ways to view familiar things in unfamiliar ways is by seeking out someone who has an opposing point of view from your own. For instance, consider the following scenario.

Scenario

Helen and Jim are coworkers involved in a conflict at work; they constantly rub each other the wrong way and hold negative opinions of the other. Helen's boss, Sam, knows Jim well and generally has a good opinion of him. Frustrated, Helen seeks out Sam as much to complain about Jim as to hear Sam's view of him.

"Sam, can I talk with you a minute about Jim?"

"Sure, what's on your mind?" Sam asks.

"Okay, I'm going to be honest with you and say I think he's a miserable little rat-faced creep."

"So, why are you coming to me?"

"Because you seem to like the little creep, and I thought maybe you could help me with my perspective. I'm trying to be open."

"You have an interesting way of being open. Now tell me why you think he's such a creep."

"Well, one day I needed extra paper for my computer at home, so I went to the supply room and slipped a couple of reams of paper into my briefcase. He saw me and said those reams of paper weren't for private use. I ignored him, but I was furious."

"Well, Helen, you might not have known this, but Jim had his own business before he came here. He lost a lot of money due to employee theft, so he's very sensitive about pilferage. He's told me a number of times how fortunate he feels to be working here. He doesn't know that you do a lot of work at home, so he probably assumed you were taking the paper for personal use."

The revelations you learn about a hated coworker usually don't make you realize he's really a saint. The point, however, is that seeing someone through another person's eyes can be eye-opening. We need to actively solicit opposing viewpoints to see situations with more depth and breadth. Otherwise, we'll continue to adhere to our old perspectives and feel powerless. After talking to Sam, Helen might possibly be more willing to approach Jim and try and develop a relationship with him. While she might never consider him a friend, she can develop an appreciation for his strengths that allows her to work more productively with him. More importantly, Helen becomes a more broad-minded person, willing to consider other perspectives before drawing a conclusion or deciding on a course of action.

My experience in mediating conflicts would indicate that rarely is either person ill intended, yet both generally view the other as such. It is only through challenging their own views that they will enable themselves to come together and resolve their conflict.

Applying Technique 3 allows us to move outside of the boxes we often create for ourselves. Thinking outside of the box is important for coming up with new solutions to problems. Bobby Layne, former NFL quarterback, once said, "I have never lost a game in my life. Once in a while time ran out on me." His quote is a great example of how a person can step out of the box and look at things quite differently.

Here's a simple exercise to put this technique to work for you. In the box provided, list someone you work with who holds very different views from you, and briefly describe how his or her views differ from yours. Keeping these different ideas in mind, invite the individual to join you for lunch or coffee. Your only goal is to listen with an open mind and suspend your negative judgment. Do you find anything worthwhile or valid in this person's ideas when you listen in this manner? Do you now have a broader view of an old problem or a familiar situation than you did before you sat down and listened to this "opposing" person?

Somebody whose view is different than mine:	
Who is it and how do they differ from me?	When and how would I like to meet with this person?

Technique 4: Identify a single thought that could change your life.

Technique 4 is based on a Chinese proverb that says a journey of a thousand miles begins with a single step. I would add the corollary that a single step begins with a single thought. A personal takeover does not start with you suddenly doing a new thing without a certain amount of reflection. Personal takeovers start in our heads, and once the thought emerges and takes hold, action will invariably follow.

Have you ever thought that you could be CEO of your company? Or that you might turn your hobby into a career? Or that you could relocate to a small town and still be successful? Or that if you added one more skill set, you would be able to have your pick of jobs?

Unfortunately, many of us are afraid to think life-changing thoughts. Some of us find them too grandiose. We chide ourselves for not being "realistic." A life-changing thought gathers tremendous weight over time, pushing us to take an action in line with that thought. Therefore, we sometimes shy away from allowing these thoughts to take hold.

Determine your capability to think a life-changing thought by deciding which of the following five choices would best fit your mood:

- What an incredible time to be alive.
- Life is pretty good, overall.
- Life has its ups and downs.
- Man, it is hard to live day to day.
- Life stinks!

The self-fulfilling prophecy

If you chose the first one, you're much more likely to countenance a life-changing thought than if you chose the last one. Numerous studies have shown that we create a Pygmalion effect or self-fulfilling prophecy through our beliefs. If you believe life stinks, then you're likely to think the type of thoughts that keep you stuck in your rut. If life stinks, you're not going to tell yourself, "I should be a poet rather than a fish wholesaler." On the other hand, if you believe this is an incredible time to be alive, you will feel sufficiently good about yourself and the world around you to venture a daring, life-altering thought.

Martin, for instance, had a very positive attitude, and it had helped him do well as a sales executive for a Fortune 500 company. But in recent years, his job had become routine. He'd helped revamp the sales department and had been promoted into an executive position. While he was well-paid and relatively secure in his job, he missed "the action." Still, Martin had been conditioned to believe that he had made the right career decision and that to second guess himself would be heresy. In the last year, however, he'd really found his job stultifying, and so he permitted himself the following thought: *I could go back to being a salesman again if I wanted.*

The thought simmered in Martin's brain for a while, and finally it heated up to the point that he started making some phone calls to friends with other companies, inquiring about openings. Eventually, he took the step of going on a few interviews "just to see what would happen." When he was offered a job at a Fortune 100 company, he accepted, knowing that he would have to take a pay cut in the beginning but convinced that eventually he would be making far more money than his current salary. More importantly, he was excited about work for the first time in more than a year and couldn't wait to start this new chapter in his life.

Scenario

The self-fulfilling prophecy affects both our professional and personal lives. Let's listen to Charlie to see how we create a self-fulfilling prophecy in our personal lives:

"I tell you, my wife is going to leave me any day now. I know she is. I can tell by the way she acts. She always seems like she wants to get away from me, acting sneaky. So I don't let her out of my sight, except when I have to go to work. But then, I'll surprise her by coming home at lunch, or I'll take a long break or leave early to see if she's home. If she isn't, I'll ask her where she's been. The other day, I caught her out and asked her where she had been. She said, 'Shopping.' I asked, 'Where's the groceries and receipts?' She said, 'I was looking at clothes.' How am I to know whether she's telling the truth? She says she loves me, but I've asked if she is 'in love' with me, and she goes blank. When we drive in the car, I can see her looking at other guys as they drive by. Sometimes I get to the point where I just want to explode."

When we listen to Becky, Charlie's wife, we hear the effects of Charlie's attention.

"It's suffocating. I married Charlie because I genuinely thought I loved him. He was good looking, smart, seemed to have all the right things going for him. I guess I overlooked his jealousy and distrust. It's like he's convinced I'm doing something behind his back, seeing someone else. I'm not, but I can't stand it. When we're together, he's watching my every move. If I even glance out of the car window and there happens to be a man walking down the street, Charlie's convinced I'm longing to be with that guy. Then Charlie starts getting himself all worked up. I can see it. He starts talking sarcastically to me or goes stone silent, brooding. It's nuts.

"I honestly don't know how long I can stay with Charlie," continues Becky. "When we're not together, and I go to the grocery store, I never know if he isn't spying on me from the next aisle. Heck, he even might have hired one of those detective firms. I wouldn't be surprised if the phone is tapped somehow. That's how jealous and suspicious he is. This behavior is stifling. I can't breathe."

How long do you think Becky is going to stay with Charlie? He might be the most handsome, wealthy, and successful person around, but odds are he'll soon be single. If Charlie had completed the previous exercise, checking off one of the statements, there's a good chance he would check the one that says, "Man, it's hard to live day to day."

You might be the reverse of Charlie. If you believe this is an incredible time to be alive and are excited about each passing day, you are much more likely to show it. Instead of spending each day in distrust and suspicion, like Charlie, you're much more likely to demonstrate optimism. Your excitement will likely electrify not only you, but others. Your life, your future, has a much greater probability of being a happy one, possibly even an incredible one, than Charlie's does.

What is a single thought that could change your life by turning a negative self-fulfilling prophecy into a positive one for you? This thought could represent a vision for yourself, like *Every day I am becoming more of a takeover thinker.* It could be far more specific, like, *I find ways daily to encourage everyone and never discourage them.* It could be related to something you now know you wish to do, like *I'm going to become a programmer.* It could be something in your personal life, like *I'm going to make that commitment to Basim to marry him.* Write it down in the box provided. Think about how your life would be different if you take this step.

A single thought that could change my life:

Technique 5: Find a way to differentiate yourself in the eyes of others at work.

When a company wants to succeed, what does it do? It looks for its competitive advantage. It looks for ways in which it can differentiate itself, so that it can be perceived positively in the market place. The same thing applies to individuals who are transitioning between the victim and takeover phases of their lives. They need to make a statement and commitment that "things have changed." Differentiating themselves achieves this objective. Individuals who are most successful have found ways to positively differentiate themselves from everyone else.

Eula works in the Post Office as a customer service representative. Though she didn't go through the formal takeover process described in this book, she obviously found a way to launch her takeover instinctively, using differentiation as a catalyst:

"I used to have a bad attitude. When the doors would open in the morning, I'd yell out 'Here come the sheep!' I'd even go 'baaah' when the first person came through the door. Well, one day even I realized I had gone too far. It was during the holiday season, and the line seemed endless. I was just finishing with this customer who began to walk away. Another fella, obviously in a hurry, quickly came over to me before I had called him over. Well, I looked at him with the meanest look I could muster and I barked, 'Back in line!' He froze in his tracks, afraid to take another step. I think he thought I was going to "go postal." Then I saw all the other faces, some with fear, some with looks of disgust. I went home that night and was really bothered by what I had done. I had gone too far. Then something happened the next morning that kind of put things in perspective.

I was off that day, so I decided to get an early start shopping. I went to the mall and arrived just as the doors were opening. Well, when I went through the doors as they were being unlocked, I heard one of the sales clerks say, 'Here come the sheep.' I was really offended. I decided that night that people shouldn't have to put up with this kind of treatment, even though I must admit that many of my coworkers also treat people in this negative way. So, now I go all out to treat people well, which is what our management keeps encouraging, but still a lot of the other clerks think it's kind of a freakish way to act.

Do you know that today my productivity is the highest in our office? I try to get those customers taken care of and on their way. Right now my goal is to take care of at least three hundred customers every day. Oh, and that guy I threatened was in the other day. I went out to the lobby while he was standing in line. I went up to him and apologized, and told him it would be a pleasure to take care of him in the future. His name's Larry and he's kinda cute."

To change her approach to people, Eula set a goal for herself. Her goal helped her differentiate herself in a positive way from the other clerks. This goal of taking care of 300 customers gave her something to focus on. Goals focused on differentiation help us create momentum: They help us move forward. Whether we look at the world of sports, business, or government, the people who are most successful are those who have differentiated themselves.

Years ago, conformity was seen as the way to get ahead. People did everything possible to avoid calling attention to themselves. Today most individuals will be overlooked if they attempt to maintain the status quo or if they choose to remain invisible. You can choose to call attention to yourself in a negative way, just as

Eula did initially, or you can shift that view, again as Eula did, and make it a positive differentiator. But differentiation is critical to enable you to be viewed as a key contributor within your organization.

A personal takeover is a truly individual act, and it helps when you have a sense of your own individuality. Differentiation helps you think of yourself as special or unique. Instead of perceiving yourself as one of the herd, you seize your difference and know that you can forge your own path. The difference that you come up with doesn't have to be monumental. You don't have to convince your coworkers that you work harder than everyone in the company or show your boss that you're more talented. It can be as simple as thinking of yourself as being a bit more empathetic than others. Or you may determine that your point of difference is a specific soft skill like communication or a technical skill like spreadsheet analysis.

It's also possible that you can't immediately think of a way that you're different. You feel your skills and personality are generally similar to others you work with. In this case, target a specific type of coworker—bosses, peers, direct-reports, suppliers, customers—and focus on how you can differentiate yourself in their eyes. You may be able to treat your direct reports with more respect than other bosses. You may decide that you want to show your bosses that you're willing to be more honest and straightforward than others.

Whatever you choose, make sure it's something that fits with who you are rather than someone you're not. Our points of difference emanate from our experience, expertise, and personality. Everyone has at least one distinct trait, skill, or area of knowledge (and often, more than one) that can be used as a point of differentiation.

In the box that follows, set a "small" differentiation goal for the next week. Make it an action that truly will differentiate you positively from everyone else. It might be something like, *I'm going to beat every deadline this week* (the difference: being faster than others) or *I'll call two customers a day to see how things are going and determine if I can help them in any way* (the difference: being more helpful to customers).

> My goal for the week—to positively differentiate me from others:

Technique 6: Say something positive about your boss, a peer, the organization, friends, or customers every day for 30 days.

It is hard to be positive day in and day out. It requires effort. It is based on the idea that if we view people positively, it is hard to have enemies. We will have more friends and people who want to support us if we, in turn, are focused on being positive about them.

Scenario

Taylor works for a road commission. He oversees crew members who repair highways 24 hours a day, 365 days a year. He's always been negative. He's always done good work, but until recently, everyone viewed him as a downer. When he walked into a room, they looked for reasons to excuse themselves. While his crew members respected his intelligence, they hated listening to his endless litany of what was wrong with

the commission. Taylor's boss, Mac, summed up how he felt about Taylor:

"Taylor was promoted before I came here. I never would have promoted the guy. Chronic complainer. Always looked for the dark side of anything. If I came to him to discuss how we might improve our work, he'd have a thousand reasons why it couldn't be done. And these reasons often were linked to statements about how the county was corrupt. It's hard to fire people in a place like this, but I had had it. I finally told him that I thought he needed to look for another job."

Taylor never expected his boss to tell him to look for another job. "At first," Taylor said, "when Mac told me to go look for another job, I was really angry. I sulked for about a month. Then others started saying the same thing to me. I guess they were sick of my behavior. It was pretty bad. I kind of prided myself on this tough exterior demeanor. Like I couldn't say anything nice to anyone. Then after sulking awhile, I realized that I didn't want another job. I also realized that I had created a lot of enemies within the road commission. I needed to change that. So I decided to talk to Mac about it."

"I couldn't believe it when Taylor approached me," said Mac. "He never showed the least interest previously in what I had to say. Now he was here, all sad, telling me he really wanted to stay. I figured this was my chance. I needed to unload on him. So I did. I told him how awful his behavior was, that he was never positive about anything. I told him I had never heard him say one nice thing about any person within the commission. He asked me what I thought he should do. I asked him if he really thought everyone was so terrible around here. He said that a lot of it was just show. It was how he talked, how he tried to create this tough image. He really couldn't get himself to say he liked people, particularly me, but he grunted 'uh huh' when I asked if maybe he thought people here weren't so bad. I told him he needed to start being more positive."

"When Mac told me to start being more positive, I really didn't know what to do," Taylor said. "I kind of made a joke about it the next day to one of the guys on the crew, but he suddenly turned on me and sarcastically said, 'Maybe you could start by acknowledging that someone other than you does something right.' That comment hit me, and I went home that night and talked to my wife about it. She agreed with Ralph, the guy on the crew. She said I never give her a compliment about anything. She said I always bad mouth the people at work. I was up all that night. A couple of times I almost decided to chuck it all, to leave the job. But I knew it meant too much to me. The next morning, I just did it. I went to see Mac. He was busy and I knew he really didn't want to see me, but I waited outside his office. Finally, he waved me in. It took all my guts to do this, because I honestly can't remember ever having done it before. I stood in front of his desk and said some words I had rehearsed all morning. I said, 'Mac, you're the best thing that ever happened to me. I'm glad you kicked me in the butt. You're a good boss, you listen, you're honest, and you're smart. The county is lucky to have you. From now on, I'm going to do my best to be the kind of team leader you can be proud of.'"

Mac was flabbergasted. "I couldn't believe my ears, and I doubted that Taylor really meant it. But sure enough, I began seeing changes in him. He began complimenting his workers. He even commended Scotty, the Road Commission Manager, on a new snow removal system Scotty was launching. Not a day goes by that Mac doesn't seem to find something good to say about someone. You have to understand how important this is to me. Before, I spent a lot of time trying to smooth over bad feelings when he'd snipe at someone. Now he's building morale instead of pulling it down."

This interview with Mac and Taylor shows how someone can shift their image and their own mental model by focusing on finding something positive each day. Here is an activity that will help shift this focus as you embark on your takeover. In the following box, identify something positive about each of the following: your boss, another employee, a customer, and your organization.

Name of individual	Something positive I can say

Whatever you write in the box should be genuinely positive. Don't get yourself in the trap of writing something cynical or making a joke out of it. For example, don't say that a positive trait about your coworker is that she sits next to the trash container, and therefore, absorbs the germs before they hit you!

Resolve that you are going to provide this feedback to one of them tomorrow, and over the next few days give this feedback to each of them. At first, this may be difficult to do. If you've been known as a cynic or feel yourself to be introverted, it may be unsettling to step out of your comfort zone. This is where Technique 2—taking a risk—becomes important. Push yourself out of that comfort zone, take the risk, and give the other person some positive feedback.

You may experience cognitive dissonance with this exercise. Cognitive dissonance occurs when you initiate an activity not believing it will have any effect. However, the results you receive cause you to see the value in the activity. So in this example, you may begin giving others positive feedback, maybe not really believing it will make any kind of a difference. You could very well, however, find that those others start responding differently to you than they have previously.

Technique 7: Replace the words
have to with *choose to* or *want to*.

This final technique is a very important technique because it allows you to continually reinforce the idea that you have choices. During the transition to takeover thinking, you need to remind yourself of this fact. As a victim thinker, you probably resorted to using the words "have to" when communicating with others. For instance, how often have you said something like, "I can't get together with you next Saturday night because I have to go to my daughter's volleyball game." The fact is you don't *have to* go to your daughter's volleyball game. You may *want to* go to your daughter's volleyball game, and as a result, you *choose to* go to your daughter's volleyball game, but you don't *have to* go.

The words *have to* are words that disempower us. By realizing that we choose to do the things we do, we are likely to not only have more energy about those things, but we will also continually empower ourselves.

Pre-takeover, most people feel that their choices are limited or that they really don't have choices at all. They believe that their lives are circumscribed by their jobs, their economic circumstances, their career goals, their education, their intelligence and many other factors. As a result, they turn down numerous opportunities and new experiences because they *have to* do something else, for instance:

- I can't accept the new job on the West Coast because I have to live on the East Coast.
- I can't go back to college and get that advanced degree I want because I have to devote all my time to my job.
- I'm not going to explore job opportunities with the best company in our industry because I have to stay here; the company depends on me.

If, in the above statements, you can replace *have to* with *want to*, then that's great. You're in control of the choices you make. On the other hand, if you find yourself turning down desirable opportunities because you have to do something you don't want to do, you're fooling yourself into believing you're a slave. Most of the time, we use *have to* as a crutch because we're scared of doing something new or different.

We also use *have to* as an excuse to get us out of doing something we don't want to do. For instance, Gene regularly used this device to get out of activities he found undesirable. In reflecting on this, Gene says, "I didn't really realize that what I was doing at the time was actually dishonest. I wasn't being honest to others or to myself. They were just little white lies. I received an invitation to the company picnic, and really didn't wish to go. I remember responding with something like, 'I'm sorry. I just can't go to the picnic. I have to go to a funeral.' Well, there wasn't any funeral, and I'm lucky nobody asked me who it was. I would have had to make up something, and it would have gotten even worse. The fact of the matter is, on that day I just wanted to kick back at home. We'd been working on a huge project, and I just didn't want to see anybody. It hit me that it would be better to tell the truth, when Sarah who works with me, was asked by Stacy, our boss, if she was going to the picnic. Guess what Sarah said. She said, 'Naw, I've seen enough of you guys. I'm going to just kick back at home.' Then Stacy agreed with her. So, here I was lying, saying I can't go because I have to do something, when I really just didn't want to go."

You'll find it's much easier to execute a personal takeover when you throw away these crutches of *I can't* or *I have to*. When you stop artificially limiting your options because of every *have to* in your life, you'll find it's that much easier to take control of your actions. It won't always be easy. Sometimes, it's hard to tell someone that you'd prefer to do something other than to be with them. Yet, if you succumb to the *have to*, you add the issue of dishonesty to your own disempowerment.

In the box that follows, write at least one *have to* statement you've made recently and resolve to revise it with a *want to* statement. For instance, "I can't go to the football game because I have to get that stupid report done by next Monday." The revision might be, "I'd love to go to the football game, but I've chosen to do the report over the weekend instead."

Have to statement:	*Want to* statement:

The seven techniques offered in this chapter, combined with the process described in the previous chapter, provide you with the starting points for your personal takeover. Each will give you the opportunity to experience what it's like to be in control, to shape your own reality, to have power. By giving you a "taste" of these things, it will be that much easier to launch your takeover. As you'll discover, it's much easier and more rewarding than you might have thought to be in charge of your life and steer it in a new and more productive direction.

Chapter 11

Takeover Situations: How to Use Your Power to Respond to Opportunities and Problems

❝❝ *Uh Oh! I think I'm in a situation here."*

WHEN YOU GO THROUGH A PERSONAL TAKEOVER, YOU TAKE back the power that is rightfully yours. We all have this power at birth, but we learn very early that if we whine, others will take care of us. The power to do for ourselves is distorted into the power to make others responsible for our happiness. As we grow up, we see other students in school complaining that their grades suck because the teacher sucks! So we join them in taking up the cry that it's the teacher's fault we can't perform.

When we get our first job, we'll probably find some of our coworkers blaming management for any of the failings of the organization. Thus, *managers* have replaced *teachers* as the people responsible for our success or the lack thereof. Only when we begin testing the takeover waters do we discover that we possess the tools to help free us from the many illusory constraints we've created for ourselves, yet have attributed to others.

If you eliminate remnants of the victim mindset and the many individual negathoughts that are so easy to gravitate toward when difficult situations arise, you'll find that you will exude a greater degree of confidence, assertiveness, accountability, risk-taking, and creativity. Be aware, though, that these qualities aren't easily acquired. Your negathoughts have been programmed into your mind since childhood. It takes great effort, along with trial and failure, to begin consistently employing the takeover mindset. As I've said previously, you won't accomplish this overnight.

Over time, however, you'll find that you have tremendous power at your disposal to deal with the myriad of situations you'll encounter. While the types of specific situations you'll face are infinite, most of us find ourselves in the same general types of situations. Let's look at the following common problems and opportunities:

- Losing your job.
- Receiving an unsatisfactory performance rating.
- Suffering a setback.
- Taking a high-risk, high-reward opportunity.
- Dealing with different types of people.
- Encouraging takeover thinking in others you don't manage.
- Challenging the challengers.

Losing your job

Jason is an engineer with a large, tier one auto supplier. He was recently informed that, due to economic conditions, the firm would lay him off. Let's hear how he has faced this situation:

"I've been with the company for 20 years. This is the second time they laid me off. The first time was 15 years ago. I was 24 at the time. I just sat around, waiting for the company to call me back. They did—two years later. The first year I was off, I basically sat around. I putzed around the house, watched a lot of television, and started putting on weight. I had a little saved, and my wife was working full time, so I just kept waiting for them to call me back. In the second year, we ran out of money, my wife left me, and I resorted to doing odd jobs, still waiting for the company to call me back. By now, I was angry with the company for laying me off and with my wife for leaving me. I somehow survived through that second year and was fortunate to be called back when things changed at the company. Although I was happy to get my job back, I returned as a pretty disgruntled employee, and it took a couple of years before I got over it.

"Today, I'm right back out on the street. Our company has had a lot of asbestos claims, and with the big drop in orders we've recently experienced from the car companies, I've been laid off again. But, I'm looking at this loss of work in a completely different light today. I have several options available to me. First of all, I can do exactly what I did the last time around—just sit back and wait to be called back. But when I did that, my self-esteem tanked, particularly after my wife left me. So, I don't plan to wait around. I have spent the last several weeks identifying my options. I could stay in engineering, but because I have a technical background, there are also possibilities in technical sales and technical training. I have assessed my skills, along with the things I like to do. There are a number of possibilities. Some probably won't pay very much, since I'll be starting out from square one. But, I think that with my experience, I'll be able to grow my salary over time. It will merely require that I adjust my living expenses to match a new level of income."

Given the volatile environments and industries many of us work in, there is the possibility we may lose our jobs at some point. When that happens, we can react angrily and lethargically, as Jason did the first time, or we can react by giving ourselves choices, as Jason did the second time around. With a takeover mindset, we can open up job and career paths for ourselves that we never even knew existed when we were in our victim state. Therefore, keep your takeover mindset firmly in place if you lose your job and you'll find you'll be able to do the following:

- **Feel and then let go of your negative emotions.** It's perfectly natural to be angry when you're told (directly or indirectly) that you're not wanted and to complain and feel sad. Takeover thinkers, however, don't wallow in these emotions. They have such a firm belief in themselves and their ability to control their fate that they move past these emotions and start replacing them with positive feelings about the future.

- **Look for the door that opens when the other door closes.** As this adage implies, negative events beget opportunities. Takeover thinkers actively look for new career paths and possibilities when they are fired. They are excited about finally having the time to investigate new jobs or industries. When they receive a sizeable severance, they see it as "pennies from heaven," realizing that this is a once-in-a-lifetime chance to fund their own business. They find that they have the energy and impetus to gather the information and make the contacts that they never had before, and they take advantage of it.

- **Become a freed lion rather than a tail-between-the-legs dog**. When takeover thinkers go on new job interviews or start networking, they don't go hat in hand like victim thinkers. They feel liberated from the constraints of a company in trouble or a boss that didn't appreciate them. They realize that this is their chance to shine and they intend to take full advantage of it. Takeover thinkers radiate energy. They walk into a room and are certain that they can help others, and job interviewers and potential customers feel this confidence and respond positively to it.

Receiving an unsatisfactory performance rating

Discussions about performance can be very emotional. We each like to feel we're doing a good job. It's not unusual for us to see our performance in a different light than someone else might. Performance reviews often involve some degree of subjectivity, and that's where we can be at odds with our boss.

Scenario

Yvonne is a supervisor within a large department store. She recently received an unsatisfactory rating on her annual performance review, due to turnover among her staff and low sales in her department. She talks about her reaction.

"I received a review last month from Tim, my boss. He's only 23 years old, and he gave me this unsatisfactory rating. So, picture this. He has to sit down with me, a woman who happens to be African-American and 47 years old, and tell me that my performance is unsatisfactory. If this were 10 years ago, I probably would have played the race, age, and gender cards. I probably would have scared the daylights out of him, and the store would have probably changed my rating.

"But what is all that going to do for me? The fact of the matter is, he was right. I have had high turnover in my department in the last year. And business has just been slow. You could roll a bowling ball through the entire store some nights and not hit a shopper. So, if I wanted to, I could scream holy murder that I was being a scapegoat or discriminated against or just being treated unfairly.

"Now, I must be honest here. I didn't just roll over and play dead when Tim told me my performance was unsatisfactory. I pointed out to him that if my performance was unsatisfactory, so was his, because he's my boss. And so is the performance of the department store manager, if the rest of the departments have such sorry sales, which I know they do. Tim tried to weasel out of it, saying that he was involved in many other things, but I told him to cut the crap. When all is said and done, the business of this store is selling stuff, and if we aren't selling, we aren't performing—none of us. Poor Tim wasn't ready to face up."

At the same time, Yvonne didn't get stuck in blaming and excuse-making. Instead, after the performance review, she went into her office and wrote out her options:

1. Stay at the company and try to get the performance rating changed.
2. Find another job.
3. Stay at the company, accept the rating, and try to improve my performance.

"I chose the third option, because I really do like the department store, and I like my job. I decided that I needed to address two things: my turnover and my shift's sales. So, I called a meeting with the sales clerks two weeks ago. We sat down and talked about the turnover. I learned some things about myself that I'm going to work on. We also talked about sales. The group came up with a whole slew of ideas on how we could get more customers into the store. I invited the store manager and Tim to a shift meeting where we presented our ideas. The store manager really liked them, and we've begun implementing several. By the way, the store manager pulled me aside after the meeting and said, 'Yvonne, you've done some great work here. I'd like you to speak at our next storewide sales meeting.'"

Yvonne's actions show her willingness to take a risk when faced with what, in many of our eyes, might seem like a patently unfair performance rating. She had a choice, and the choice she took was to focus on what she could learn and how she could improve the performance of her group. Is there a chance that she will not be successful in raising her shift's sales? Of course. At the same time, her personal stock in the company has increased tremendously in the eyes of the store manager.

If you're faced with a negative performance review—or any type of criticism from a boss or a customer—use your takeover thinking to take the following actions:

- **Remind yourself that you have a choice.** You can accept the negative review—whether or not it was deserved—and determine what you need to do to improve it; you can challenge the review, or you can make the choice to explore other positions. Takeover thinkers always have the power to improve; they realize they control the review and the review does not control them.

- **Should you stay in the same job, focus considerable energy on getting new things done rather than defending your old actions.** Be energized by the review; let it catalyze all sorts of meetings, proposals, and projects that address the alleged problem identified by the review. Don't waste energy on defending your past actions (either to yourself or someone else), but apply it to achieve specific goals.

Suffering a setback

At some point or another, all of us suffer personal setbacks that can affect our work directly or indirectly. It may be a divorce, problems with children, financial woes, or physical illness.

Let's look at how Tom, an individual with a strong takeover mentality, dealt with a serious illness.

"I distinctly remember throwing the football around with my two boys on Thanksgiving Day in 1997. We were having great fun playing touch football with their cousins while dinner was cooking. Dinner turned into the usual happy, big family event that Thanksgiving should be. I became famous for the toast I made at dinner, 'To family who are like friends, and friends who are like family.' I was a pretty happy guy. I had a loving family, a successful business, an active lifestyle, which included playing on an over 30 indoor soccer team, weekly racquetball or golf games with friends, and watching and coaching my boys in their athletic pursuits.

"The next morning we went up to our cottage in Ontario. At dinner time, I noticed a pain spreading into my right arm. I attributed it to pulling a muscle the day before in our family football game. However, by the next morning it had worsened to a burning pain in both my arms and neck. Within hours I was bedridden and wracked with pain. My wife, Karen, took me to a chiropractor to see if I had a pinched nerve, and we visited the local emergency room where we received a prescription of muscle relaxers. Neither relieved the symptoms. On Sunday, I was racked with pain in my arms, back, and legs. My family rigged up a 'bed' in the back of our van and we headed back to Michigan for some more comprehensive care. It was a grueling five-hour trip with every bump and vibration and bounce causing me extreme grief. I was trying to be a 'good soldier' for my family, but the pain was agonizing.

"Over the course of the next two days I had an MRI, doses of heavier muscle relaxers, and another chiropractic visit with no change in my condition. The pain, at this point, had become constant and overwhelming. I was feverish, I could not sleep, I could not think, I could not maintain any show of strength. In fact, I fully believe I understood the motivation that Dr. Kevorkian's patients would have had to end it all.

"Wednesday morning, I lost the ability to move my legs. We called an ambulance, and after a painful ride to the local hospital, I was suddenly receiving urgent attention from several doctors trying to figure out what was causing my symptoms. After several hours and a merciful morphine drip into my arm, a diagnosis was confirmed. An abscess had formed inside my spinal cord on the front of my C6 vertebrae. It was osteomyelitis, a *staphylococcus aureus* infection growing at a fast rate. It was growing inside a layer of cells that was protecting my body the best way possible, however it was just a matter of time before the cell layer broke and the infection was going to be unstoppable. I was near death!

"I only know the rest from later stories, as I was in a morphine haze. People were shadows around me. A skilled neurosurgeon was called in. He and an orthopedic surgeon were going to operate on my spinal column, to eliminate the offending abscess by removing the front of my C6 vertebrae and replacing it with part of my hipbone. An IV of some of the strongest antibiotics was started. Karen was informed that the odds of survival of the surgery were very low, the odds of survival without surgery were nil, and the odds of my walking again following surgery were only 50/50.

"The surgery was successful in saving my life. Thank God for the skill of my doctors. I don't remember much of the next few days in the ICU. I woke up in one of those braces that people with broken necks have to wear. Karen shaved the hair on my head to minimize the care it would need. I slept a lot. What I remember is that one day, about a week later, I was able to create a twitch in my right foot. The next day I could move my left foot. A few days later, two physical therapists showed up and made me stand up. Bless their hearts, they made me walk two or three steps the next day. One of my doctors came by one day and saw me in a wheel chair on the rehabilitation therapy floor. He checked me over and said, 'You're going to be all right!' It was the most encouragement I had received in the weeks I had been in the hospital. Various therapists, including Andrea, Laura, and Gloria made me work my arms and legs and conditioned me to regain some of my capabilities over the next few months. They are angels.

"While recuperating, I felt an aura of goodwill from the people around me and somehow from within myself. It was like a bright light shining on me and from me. I was a willing participant in my recuperation process. But this light, this energy, gave me additional strength. When Laura wanted me to do 10 pulls on one of the workout machines I would do twelve. When she asked for 10 minutes on the treadmill I would try to do 11.

"My recuperation during 1998 was dramatic from the low point I had been at in December 1997. It was a long road. I started going back to my sons' athletic and school events. I ended up selling out of my business and backing off from many of my life's activities. Not everything is perfect today in my system, but I am thankful for what I have, for every day and every minute.

"In the summer of 2002, I decided to take a two day, 150-mile bike ride for charity. I took on the ride as a challenge to continue my recovery process. The first two miles were great! All downhill. I hit the 'wall,' however, at mile 20. At that point, my will had to take over from my physical body. Intellectually, that made sense, but that did not make it easier. I forced myself through it and found myself caught up with my friend, Gerry, at mile 25, and back to a decent pace.

"The final 30 miles in the first day were grueling and uneventful except for pain, and the frustration of the course being longer than 75 miles. It turned into 80. Doesn't seem like much of a difference unless you just rode 75 miles. Five extra miles at that point is an extra 30 minutes on the bike, on the seat, in the heat, with a sore neck. Very frustrating! However, **we did it**! I have to admit that my neck was causing me great pain at that point, and all I wanted to do was lie down.

"We checked into our rooms and I crashed from the day's effort. Gerry rang my room to wake me up for dinner, and I crashed again right after that. The next morning I rose with a lot of doubts about how my neck was going to handle the first 10 miles. Actually, the first 10 miles were fine, except it was hotter than Saturday and there were more bugs. The neat thing about a bike though is that the faster you go the cooler it feels, and at the same time the bugs get farther down your throat where they don't bother you as much because they are easier to swallow. At about mile 15 my neck started to pinch again. Gerry's feet were going numb, so we made quite a pair. Grunt and Groan were probably good nicknames. I really shouldn't say that, Gerry really didn't complain at all. I complained enough for both of us. We nearly quit three different times. We would quit. Then we would start again. Then quit again. Then start again.

"There is nothing quite like the rush of crossing the finish line for an event like this where you have pushed yourself well beyond your limits. It is truly one of the most exciting things I have ever participated in, from an

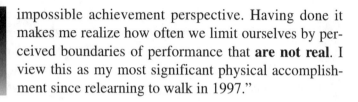

impossible achievement perspective. Having done it makes me realize how often we limit ourselves by perceived boundaries of performance that **are not real**. I view this as my most significant physical accomplishment since relearning to walk in 1997."

Obviously, some setbacks are easier to overcome than others. Tom's involved the near loss of life and giving up his position as President of a well-known training firm. He had many choices to make during his long, tough road to recovery. At each step along the way, he could have decided to give up his fight for recovery. Yet, he didn't. He realized the choices available to him and the consequences of any decision he might make. Many of us would have given up when faced with everything Tom faced. That's what characterizes his personal takeover. Tom's story represents a nonprofessional comeback. You can apply the same takeover thinking to whatever setback you face.

If you find yourself trying to recover from some difficult event in your life, use the following takeover tactics:

- **Don't feel sorry for yourself**. Admittedly, it can be difficult to follow this advice after a serious illness or other major personal problem, but takeover thinkers have amazing resilience to draw upon. Focus on everything you have rather than whatever you've lost. Give yourself ambitious goals like Tom did and pursue them with gusto.

- **Remove illusory boundaries**. Your setback has probably imposed all sorts of limits in your mind. The emotional or physical trauma you suffered makes you think you'll never be the same again. It's natural to feel like this at first, but if you are a true takeover thinker, you'll fight the urge to think this way. Try to tear down the fictitious boundaries with the power of your thoughts. Your mindset is critical to your recovery. As Tom's story shows, you have enormous personal power if you choose to recognize it. Use this knowledge to move forward without any restrictive limits.

Taking a high-risk, high-reward opportunity

Opportunities can be scary, which is why victim thinkers tend to see all the negative permutations of what seems like a positive experience. Takeover thinkers, on the other hand, recognize that opportunities carry risk, but trust in their ability to manage the risk in order to have a chance at the reward. As a result, they not only handle opportunities better than victim thinkers but they do more with them. Let's look at how one person dealt with her negathoughts and applied takeover thinking to overcome initial doubts and fears about an opportunity that presented itself.

Roxanne is a customer service representative at a medical claims firm. Her manager, Anita, was scheduled for surgery that would involve a recovery period of three months. Here's how Roxanne described what happened:

"When Anita first approached me about her surgery, I felt bad for her. Three months of pain and recuperation is not my idea of a good time. Then she lowered the boom and told me she'd like me to cover for her. I gasped. You just have to know me. I'm a good worker, but I've never been one to give orders to people. I just like to do my job. She told me that I'd be acting supervisor while she was gone. Then she told me something even more frightening. She said she'd like me to take the test the state gives to certify medical administrators. Well, I was a decent student in school, but I was just as happy to get out. I mean, I threw all my books into the trashcan at school at the end of each semester, and I never liked tests—I kind of freeze up when I take them.

"My first reaction was to not see this as any kind of opportunity at all—except maybe an opportunity to make a lot of friends mad at me, and maybe even be fired. We've got more than 60 people here. Some are a lot older than me, but I like just about all of them. I just couldn't see myself giving them orders. Some of them are more qualified than me; they've been here longer, and they'd probably resent me getting this opportunity. I actually kind of resented that Anita had put me in this position of having to say no to her.

"Then, this thing with the test. My mind raced with negative thoughts. *What if I fail it? I don't want to take the time to study for this test. Won't people think I'm a dummy when I come back having failed it? And then, when I try to give them assignments, why are they going to listen to me?* The more I thought about this, the angrier I became. Why was I singled out? So, I went to Anita and told her I wouldn't do it. She asked me to just think about it for a few days. We left it at that.

"A few days later, I was approached by Ophelia. She's like the grand dame of the service representatives. She's been here the longest, really knows medical claims, and she's got to be in her late 60s. She told me that she had heard that Anita asked me to cover for her. I told Ophelia that I had declined the assignment. Ophelia shocked me when she said, 'Are you nuts? Why haven't you jumped on this opportunity?'

"I started to tell her all the reasons I shouldn't do it, like how I couldn't manage someone like her, with all her experience, and how I freeze when I take tests. She told me I was just limiting myself. 'Why not see if there isn't a positive side to this?' she asked me. Ophelia told me that I was making the consequences too severe. I told her that people would laugh at me when they found out I failed the test. She jumped on that and said that most of them would be afraid to take the test, and the worst that could happen is that I got a low score. And even if I got a 45, I'd still have learned more in studying for the test than most people in the claims unit currently know. I really hadn't thought about it this way. Ophelia then let me in on a secret. She told me it took Anita three times before she passed the test.

"Okay, I countered. I'll grant you that I can learn something by taking the test, and it might be fun to give myself this kind of a challenge. But how am I going to order someone like you around? I asked her. She just laughed and asked me if I had studied management under Attila the Hun. Ophelia put her arm around me and told me that the best managers are those that serve others. They don't order people around. She said all I would have to do is tell the group that I'd be doing the best I could. She said to not worry about those who grumble about me getting the opportunity instead of them. If I wanted to, I could tell everyone that I know some of them might feel they should have been given the opportunity, and probably some of them are more deserving. But I could just say that I was going to do the best that I can.

"As Ophelia talked to me, she made more and more sense. After a few more discussions with her, I decided to take on the challenge. I studied for the test. It was the toughest exam I ever took. I barely squeaked by, but I did it!

"I decided that I was going to be kind of coordinating the group's efforts instead of managing them. This different way of looking at things really worked out for me. There were a few people who resented me for getting the opportunity, but for the most part, people were pretty okay with it. In fact, when Anita came back, people told her what a good job I had done. They are now looking at me for an evening supervisor position, and I think I might try it out."

The first challenge for Roxanne was to confront her own negathoughts. With Ophelia's help, she worked through the worst possible consequences and also identified the upsides of taking this assignment. Roxanne took on the challenge, willing to risk other employees' feelings of resentment toward her, and also willing to risk failing the test. Her willingness to step out of her comfort zone and take a risk led to new opportunities. It first required a shift of mindset (with Ophelia's help), followed by the willingness to take action. If you're faced with a similar opportunity, keep the following points in mind:

- **Take control of the opportunity.** Recognize that opportunities are tremendously scary if you feel you don't have control of the situation. Until Roxanne realized that she could manage her risk and increase her chances of getting the reward, she was paralyzed by fear. By seeing how you can shape the opportunity, you can exert a significant amount of influence over where the opportunity takes you.

- **Look for the positives in your worst-case scenarios**. Ophelia helped Roxanne realize that even her worst fears had an upside. As a takeover thinker, you should be able to moderate your own fears by recognizing that there are opportunities within opportunities. Even if you don't achieve your original goal, you may benefit in all sorts of other ways. If you apply for a top position in your company and don't get it, you'll at least have alerted management to your desire to move up. If you spend a year working on a big project and it ultimately fails to receive funding, you will have established some great relationships with other people who worked on the project, and that will serve you well in the coming years.

Dealing with different types of people

Some of the greatest stress we experience as individuals within the workplace comes not from the work but from other individuals. If you think about it, you'll realize that it's the rare day when you don't have some sort of conflict with a coworker, vendor, or customer. That's because all of us come to work with our own personal baggage: the beliefs, biases, and values that we discussed earlier. These different views can lead to disagreements or to actions taken by one person that may annoy another. We each have different personality styles and different ways of going about our work. Some of us are direct and to the point. Others are very diplomatic with their language. Some of us are action-oriented and don't want to spend too much time thinking about anything. Others of us are very analytical and don't want to make a move without analyzing potential consequences. All of these differences affect our views of one another. Even with all the talk about diversity in recent years, the fact is that most of us tend to like people who are just like us. The more different you are from me, the more difficult it is to like and respect you.

A takeover mindset provides us with the capacity to deal with people who are different from ourselves. It makes us more empathetic and tolerant. Unlike victims, we aren't constantly suspicious about other people's motives, especially those individuals who think and work in very different ways from the way that we do.

Scenario

Trevor, for instance, is a budding takeover thinker in transition from his former victim mindset. He is an accountant and has been assigned to a new audit team. The team leader is Jenny, a person who started at the firm about the same time as Trevor. She graduated from a less prestigious school than Trevor, but somehow has been promoted quickly within the firm. Just

as significantly, Jenny's work style was different; she was much more open and direct than Trevor. Here's how he described his initial feelings:

"At first, I couldn't believe it when I heard Jenny got the job. I was kind of a basket case. I figured she must have pictures of somebody in a compromising position or worse. I just couldn't accept that she made it through brains and good, solid work. That is, until I began to report to her. She is the one who helped me see how my own thinking has held me back at the firm.

"When I first began reporting to her, I avoided her. Apparently she noticed, because she asked me to lunch one day. When we went to lunch, she said, 'You don't like me very much, do you?' I kind of lied and said it wasn't about liking her. I just hadn't seen anything that caused me to see her as a manager. She asked me to give her a little slack, maybe six months, and then she'd be interested in hearing if my view of her had changed. She also said that we'd be working together during the next six months, so she'd also try to share her perceptions of me.

"Well, it didn't even take six months! On our first assignment, I was complaining about how the client's records were in terrible disarray. She listened and didn't argue with me. Instead, Jenny said something like, 'I see this all the time. Don't you?' I agreed that I did. She said, 'I decided I wasn't going to let messy records upset me. In fact, I kind of shifted my reaction by realizing that we get a nice hourly fee, so if the clients want to pay us all this money to help them clean up their records, it just makes our team more profitable. I also found that it gives me some extra time with the clients, so that I can develop closer consultative relationships with them.' Jenny then told me about a bunch of opportunities she had uncovered for us with this current client that she had discovered only a few days prior.

"My respect for her only continued going up from there. She has challenged me every time I have been negative. She's shown me a totally new perspective about things. Now I'm finding ways to make the work I do more interesting, and I've been developing much better relations with my clients."

Trevor's view of Jenny changed due to his relationship with her. He started out feeling negative about her, but due to her willingness to engage him and her effective coaching, he began seeing her view of things. Jenny displayed takeover behavior when confronted with Trevor's initial disrespect. As a result of her behavior, Trevor's respect for Jenny has grown, and he is slowly moving closer to a personal takeover.

If you find yourself dealing with people different from yourself, use the following takeover methods:

- **Remind yourself that "different" doesn't necessarily mean "worse."** Rise above your prejudices and accept that people can be just as effective as you in work situations, even though they might not have the same leadership, management, or work style. Pay attention to what these different people actually say and do and judge them based on their results rather than how they say and do things. As a takeover thinker, you are capable of accommodating all sorts of personalities and styles.

- **Keep in mind that your tremendous personal power means that other people aren't a threat.** One of the reasons we sometimes have difficulty with new bosses, coworkers, or direct-reports is that they appear to be real threats; they appear to want our jobs, to get rid of us, or they seem to be in competition with us for a great position. In most instances, the enormity of these threats has been created in our own heads. When we feel weak, when we feel like victims, then we magnify small differences in philosophy and work style into major issues. Takeover thinkers understand that their power allows them to be gracious toward all sorts of other people and extend trust to them until they prove they don't deserve it.

Encouraging takeover thinking in others you don't manage

What if you are in a situation where you work or live with someone who displays an inordinate amount of victim thinking? How would you go about helping them, should you choose to do so?

Vicky works for a not-for-profit organization. She talks about her personal experience of encouraging takeover thinking in others:

I really didn't begin wanting to change other people around me. It was just because I cared about the clients. I started at the agency a few years ago while attending community college. I grew up in a migrant worker family. We'd go to Washington every year to pick apples. We'd get paid by the case. Everyone in the family would help. You needed to, if you wanted to make enough to live. I saw everything you can imagine while growing up in migrant worker communities. Life is tough, and life for migrant workers is the toughest. But you know what? You learn to survive. That's what my family did.

Eventually I landed a job at the agency. It was very difficult when I started. We deal with folks who are on the verge of becoming homeless. They've either been out of work for long periods, or continually lose jobs, often due to illness, alcohol, or drugs. When I started here, I just grabbed the work and took hold.

But I didn't get along very well with the rest of my peers. The people who work here are all well educated, with bachelor's and master's degrees. They're different from me. They're all older than me. And at first it seemed as if they were all so negative. I mean, we're supposed to be helping people here. These homeless people rely on our assistance. Yet, my peers were pessimistic about everything we were trying to do. It's like they didn't believe these people were really going to rise above their homeless situations. And they were pretty disrespectful of the agency management.

I was very unhappy and, at first, thought I was going to just quit. But as I pondered it more, I knew I had started working here for a reason. We can really help people through this agency. It was up to me to try to make a difference. So I decided to challenge others when they were being fatalistic, or when they were showing disdain for the very people we're here to support.

At first it just didn't work. I was too blunt and argumentative. If someone said something negative, I'd jump all over them. Once I pushed them, they'd push right back. My relations with the rest of the staff fell into the pits. I remember one evening, sitting at home crying, asking myself if this wasn't just a no-win situation, and dreading the return to work the next day. I decided to tell my boss, Jake, that I was going to quit.

When I went to see Jake the next day, he was very understanding. He said it didn't have to be this way for me. I asked him what he meant by that, and he said that my intentions are good, but my delivery is bad. He said he'd love to see some of the staff be a lot less negative about our clients and about the agency, and I could help them change their views, but I had to do it in a more supportive, only slightly confrontational way. We spent several hours talking about how my approach could change, and I decided to test out a new approach.

My opportunity came a few days later with Mandy, another caseworker. It was a Friday, and Mandy, who shares an office with me, stormed in and plunked down at her desk. She was clearly fuming.

"This place really sucks," she said.

"What happened?" I asked

"I just had an unexpected opportunity to go to New York, and Jake is giving me a hard time about it, because I won't be back until next Wednesday. Two lousy work days, and Jake is having a cow. Shows how much you're appreciated around here! I'll just call in sick. They can't do anything about it if I'm sick. It'll serve them right, the way they take advantage of us."

When Mandy talked about not being appreciated and how they take advantage of us, it kicked in—I knew then that she was into victim thinking. This was my opportunity to try a different tack than I had in the past.

"This doesn't sound like Jake to me, Mandy. How did you approach him about this long weekend?"

"I just told him that I had this unexpected opportunity to go to New York and I'd be back on Wednesday," Mandy replied.

"Did you just tell him you were going, or did you ask him if you could go?"

"I told him," she said.

I asked her, "And how did he respond?"

"He was kind of taken aback. I could tell he was upset."

"I guess I would be kind of upset if you just told me you were going and didn't bother to ask me. Wouldn't you be upset if you were Jake?"

"No, because I respect that people have their own personal lives," Mandy replied.

"Jake is usually a pretty reasonable guy, especially if you didn't have a lot of client appointments scheduled. Was your calendar pretty free?"

"No, but what's the difference? It's not like I don't see my clients regularly!"

Mandy was becoming defensive, and this is where I guess I would have normally taken on a persecutor role and told her off, because these clients are sometimes in dire straits.

"I can see that you're upset, Mandy. I'll bet you Jake is upset, too. Is there another way you could have approached this that would have yielded a different result, like, maybe showing Jake how you can take care of your clients later in the week?"

"He asked me about that, but then I'd have to work overtime, and because they don't pay me for overtime, I'm not going to let them take advantage of me," replied Mandy.

Mandy's narrow, self-centered view made me want to scream, but I realized that if I jumped on her now, I'd lose her.

"Mandy, don't you think you're asking for a lot here? You went in and told Jake you're taking off without giving him any recourse. You didn't offer him an alternative, like that you're willing to see your clients later in the week, or even that you've found some other caseworkers who are willing to cover for you. You just dropped this on him. Then he reacted in what seems to me a very normal and responsible way."

"Jake's put me in a real predicament. I told my friends that I'd go to New York. Now I have to call them and cancel."

"You don't *have* to do anything," I challenged. "As I see it, you have at least three choices. Your first alternative is to cancel the trip like you just said. Your second is to find a way to cover your appointments, convince Jake that you have them covered, and ask if you can have those days off. A third alternative is to go to New York and deal with whatever consequences arise as a result of that decision."

The discussion went on from there, with Mandy eventually choosing to work overtime to meet with her clients. She met with Jake, and together they worked out a plan that enabled her to go to New York. I haven't yet converted her from her victim mindset, but I am getting better at helping her without rescuing her or acting like a persecutor.

Vicky's situation shows how difficult it can be to help others change their mindsets. She had to refrain from being overly confrontational with Mandy, knowing that if she was, Mandy would only shut out Vicky's ideas.

When attempting to help others change their mindsets, think of the following:

- **Shifting from the victim mindset to the takeover mindset is a long, arduous process.** You have the advantage over those who have a lot of negathoughts in that you have learned how those negathoughts can disempower them. But they don't see it. It takes time and relentless effort on your part to help them see how they do have control over their lives.

- **Be constantly aware of when you are shifting into a persecutor or rescuer role.** It is easy to become exasperated with those who continually exhibit the victim mindset. The chronic complainer can drive you crazy. It requires that you be diligent in maintaining the takeover approach, challenging their negathoughts in a positive way, and helping them see the choices available to them.

Challenging the challengers

Be aware that not everyone will accept your personal takeover. As you change who you are, you will find yourself faced with skeptics, cynics, and other victim thinkers who have difficulty accepting your new approach to work. When I was doing my doctoral work at George Washington University, my dissertation focused on the study of a large urban high school. I had been studying a business education partnership and its impact on the students. As I interviewed the students, asking them what they planned to do, the issue of others attempting to hold them back continually turned up. One student really stood out for me. He wanted to study architecture and told me how much he loved reading about the great architects like Frank Lloyd Wright. Then he told me about his friends. "They make fun of me if they see me with a book about architecture. They say, 'Man, you're just like us. You ain't goin' nowhere.' I really want to make something of myself, but my friends are trying to hold me back. I can't let them do it. They don't want me to go to college. They want me to be just like them."

This young man is an example of the many young men and women who are trying to better their lives. In cases like his, they may have grown up in an area that is economically depressed. Instead of trying to promote them and celebrate their successes, their friends try to keep them from getting ahead.

The same thing happens to many of us when we try to change and launch our takeovers. When we try to change, our bosses, direct-reports, and fellow associates will often attempt to stop us. It is as if the negative person they know is somehow better than the positive person they don't know. Be prepared, therefore, to use your power to resist the entreaties of these takeover challengers.

Sharon has been a barely adequate supervisor. She works in a bank. She started there as a teller, about five years ago, and was promoted to Assistant Manager about two years ago because of her strong customer following. As a supervisor she has, frankly, struggled. She hasn't been able to delegate, so the customers line up at her desk in the front office, waiting to see her. Often they have transactions that any teller could handle, but due to the long-standing relationship with Sharon, they are willing to wait in line to spend a few minutes with her.

Unfortunately, up until about six months ago, if you were to walk into the branch on any given day, you would have seen Sharon up front, obviously in a harried state, trying to take care of a customer, while a line of five or six more stand outside her office. At the same time, there would be little to no line for the tellers. And the tellers would spend their time grumbling to one another about how bored they are, about how Sharon needs to learn how to delegate and about how badly she talks to them.

As Sharon would finish with a customer, she'd hurry to the back office behind the teller windows. Typically, she would throw the transaction into one of the windows with a statement like, "Don't you people have anything to do? Why am I the one who is always doing all of the work?" Then she would scamper back up to the front to take care of her next customer, and the tellers would grumble even more.

Six months ago, Sharon attended a supervisory training program. Much emphasis was placed on the art of delegation. Sharon realized during this training that her inability to delegate was creating huge problems, not only for her, but for her staff. She was becoming physically and mentally exhausted due to the constant pressure of attending to all those customers and continually facing an under-motivated staff. The staff's morale within her branch of the bank was at an all-time low. So she returned from the training all ready to begin delegating, but it didn't go so well.

On the first day after the training, Sharon decided that if a customer approached her with a transaction a teller could handle, she'd greet the customer, exchange a few pleasantries, and then walk the customer over to a teller window and introduce them. She would then ask the teller to assist the customer. Her first attempt at delegation went something like this:

"Hello Mrs. Marcos. How can I help you today?" asked Sharon.

"I'd like to wire some money to my brother in the Philippines. He needs another $50,000 for his shoe store. Got to keep it going. I get free shoes from him every couple of months."

"I see," said Sharon, "they're beautiful shoes. Why don't you come with me over to Mary Beth here, and we'll see if she can't take care of you." She walked the customer over to Mary Beth's window. Mary Beth had a bored expression on her face. This expression didn't change when Sharon introduced her to Mrs. Marcos.

Sharon said, "Mrs. Marcos, I'd like you to meet Mary Beth." No expression on Mary Beth's face. "Mary Beth, Mrs. Marcos here wishes to wire $50,000 to her brother in the Philippines. I told her you could handle this for her."

With a deadpan expression on her face, Mary Beth looked at Sharon and said, "I don't remember how to do that. I've never sent money to the Philippines before, and the last time I did a wire, it came back and you had to fix it."

Mrs. Marcos was now suddenly embarrassed, and Sharon was flustered. She tried to recoup by saying, "Oh, I'm sorry Mrs. Marcos. Come on up front and I'll take care of the wire for you." They went up front. After they were out of earshot, Mary Beth remarked to the next teller, "Now she thinks she can dump all of her work on me."

In Sharon's case, it took a number of months before she was finally able to successfully use the delegation skills she learned. Even though the tellers complained about her lack of delegation, once she began doing it, they now complained that she was dumping work on them. She also tried to change the tone in her voice as she talked with the tellers. This too was resisted. "She's being phony," said one teller. "She really doesn't mean to be nice. She can't—it's not in her nature. She really doesn't like us." All of these statements continued to occur for quite some time.

Sharon had to challenge them. As she became more of a takeover thinker, she was able to do so successfully by being authoritative without being arbitrary or overly critical. She "modeled" the behavior she expected from them. Sharon was highly conscious of acting in a responsible, compassionate manner, while also demanding accountability. She learned how to "walk the talk" and made sure that there weren't any discrepancies between what she asked her people to do and what she did. In a very real way, her actions challenged the tellers by saying to them: This is how I am because I believe it's the right way to be.

How do you challenge the challengers? Consider the following:

- **Change yourself, and be consistent about the changes.** The challengers will try to keep you exactly as you are. It's important to persevere, to be tenacious. Nothing impresses other people more than consistently practicing new behaviors. Using your takeover traits in all sorts of situations, over a sustained period of time, will communicate to others that you're serious and that there's nothing they can do to restore the "old" you.
- **Break out of your old groups**. It's tough to challenge the challengers if you lack support. It may be that you need to network and form new relationships with

people, inside and outside of your organization, who will reinforce your takeover mindset. If your inner circle is filled with skeptics and pawns, then you're going to have difficulty when people start challenging your new approach. If, on the other hand, you have people you can talk to about the flack you're receiving, you're much more likely to be resolute in how you deal with the challengers.

As you may have noticed, most of the situations I've discussed in this chapter take place in organizational settings. Just about everyone who has engaged in a personal takeover has had to learn how to shift their own mindsets, while also attempting to influence others within their organizations. Many of the tools and examples provided throughout this book can support you as you attempt to help those you care about, both within the workplace and without. Achieving your own personal takeover is not a job done in a vacuum. It requires expending some energy in challenging the negathoughts of bosses, peers, subordinates, and customers. Hopefully, through your efforts, these others will begin the journey toward their own personal takeovers.

Epilogue

The Choice You Make Right Now Will Determine Your Future

THIS BOOK HAS BEEN ABOUT THE MOST IMPORTANT TAKEOVER IN the world—your personal takeover. Nothing, however, is going to change unless you take the first step. If you simply nod your head and reflect on how takeover thinking makes sense, but fail to implement the ideas and techniques discussed in this book, nothing will change for you. A personal takeover doesn't happen by magic. It doesn't happen if you tell yourself some day you'll put all you've just learned into practice, but that you're not quite ready to do so. It won't take place if you don't make a mental and emotional commitment to the takeover process.

To give yourself the impetus to take action, think about what you've discovered about the mindsets you hold today about the world, about work, about other people, and about yourself. Think about how these mindsets impact your actions. You've seen how negathoughts completely disempower you; you've discovered various types of victim mindsets, and which ones apply to you.

At the same time, you've learned you have an alternative: the takeover mindset. You've been armed for this takeover with the tools and rules found throughout the book. From the 12-step process for converting your negathoughts to the seven jump-start techniques for shifting your mindset, you're ready to possess power over your work and career—power you now know is within your reach.

The world is not going to wait for you. It is changing in ways that most of us don't even understand. It's not inconceivable that within a decade we could have cloned humans, humans with computer chip implants, and battles with nanotechnology. We'll have a world economy where huge companies can suddenly emerge or plunge into bankruptcy due to new technologies, creative accounting, or even terrorism. We can't control any of that, and as a result, we'll likely see more people feeling like victims than ever before. In light of this, we observe our final takeover rule.

☑ Takeover Rule #20: ☑

The world around you will continue changing, whether you like it or not. You can fight it, or you can jump on and enjoy the ride.

You've finished the book. You now have a choice to make. You can succumb to the forces outside of you and just give up. Or you can take control of your future. You understand now. You've been given a key that unlocks your destiny. You don't have to live conditionally or jump through other people's hoops. You understand that your mindset today is determining your future, and if you wish to change your future, you merely have to change that mindset.

What's the next step going to be for you?

Appendix

The Takeover Rules

Takeover Rule #6:
"You can never make everyone happy. Choose the
actions that are right for you, accepting that there
will always be someone ready to criticize you." .... page 53

Takeover Rule #7:
"If you look at the world through the lens of the
victim, things will probably look pretty bleak. If you
are living your life conditionally, you are jumping
through a lot of hoops. Yelp, Yelp!" .... page 85

Takeover Rule #8:
"Don't look to others to take care of your problems." ... page 93

Takeover Rule #9:
"Don't live your life today based upon memories
from the past." .... page 96

Takeover Rule #10:
"Recognize when you are a participant in a drama
triangle and consciously step out of that role." .... page 101

Takeover Rule #11:
"Moving on to takeover thinking requires letting go
of the anger you feel toward others." .... page 102

Takeover Rule #12:
"Each negathought you replace with a positive
alternative will have a dramatically positive effect
on your future." .... page 113

Takeover Rule #13:
"True empowerment, true success, comes about as
a result of a genuine sense of well-being. The search
for material accomplishment or material gains as an
attempt to achieve well-being, often accomplishes
the opposite." .... page 118

Takeover Rule #14:
"If you believe you have options, there will always
be a way out of even the most difficult situation." .... page 127

Takeover Rule #15:
"Your mindset is the most important factor in your
success or failure—far more important than the
economy, luck, or other people." .... page 130

Takeover Rule #16:
"If you wish to achieve a personal takeover and
become more self-empowered, merely increase the
frequency with which you act self-empowered." ..... page 135

Takeover Rule #17:
"Acquiring the takeover mindset requires accepting
responsibility for the choices you make, no matter
how they may turn out." .... page 141

Takeover Rule #18:
"If you want to achieve a personal takeover,
it requires action." .... page 174

Takeover Rule #19:
"The only things preventing you from changing
your life are your own self-imposed and largely
illusory limitations." .... page 182

Takeover Rule #20:
"The world around you will continue changing,
whether you like it or not. You can fight it, or you
can jump on and enjoy the ride." .... page 242

Bibliography

Karpman, Stephen. "Fairy Tales and Script Drama Analysis." *Transactional Analysis Bulletin*, Vol. 7, no. 26, pp. 39-43. 1968.

Lewis, Cynthia Copeland. *Really Important Stuff My Kids Have Taught Me*. New York: Workman Publishing, 1994.

Moawad, Bob. *Whatever It Takes*, Edmonds, WA: Compendium, Inc., 1995. (The Wayne Gretzky and Bobby Layne quotes can be found in this book.)

Index

About the Author

G ARY IS THE PRESIDENT OF GREAT LAKES STRATEGIES AND a cofounder of Infinite Learning. Infinite Learning provides a complete training solution for organizations seeking to help their employees achieve personal takeovers. It also provides training programs in the areas of leadership, customer service, team effectiveness, and quality. Infinite Learning has offices in Akron, Denver, Detroit, and Toronto.

Gary regularly speaks to groups throughout the United States on the subject of takeover thinking. He has personally trained thousands of people, primarily in the areas of leadership and sales. He has worked with more than 200 CEOs, helping them build high-performing teams. In 2001, Gary was selected as Michigan Entrepreneur of the Year in Service Companies.

Gary has a Doctorate in Human Resource Development from The George Washington University, Washington, D.C.